An introduction to

Incarnational Spirituality

D1028836

David Spangler

An introduction to
Incarnational Spirituality

Edited by Julia Spangler
Book Design by Jeremy Berg

Published by Lorian Press
2204 E Grand Ave.
Everett, WA 98201

ISBN-10: 0-936878-37-1
ISBN-13: 978-0-936878-37-9

Spangler/David
An Introduction to Incarnational Spirituality/David Spangler

First Edition July 2011

Printed in the United States of America

0 9 8 7 6 5 4 3 2 1

www.lorian.org

Dedication

This book is dedicated to all my students over the years who helped me--and continue to help me--research and refine the deeper processes of incarnation and the practical power of Incarnational Spirituality.

Acknowledgements

Incarnational Spirituality is the result of a collaboration of minds and hearts across the vibrational threshold between the physical and non-physical dimensions of Earth with the intent of enhancing the wholeness of this world. I am deeply grateful for the consultation, information, insights, and partnership that I have enjoyed with numerous subtle beings and non-physical colleagues. That we incarnates have a deeper understanding of the nature of incarnation and the processes by which we come to this world is most important to them. It is a vital step forward in their efforts to ensure a higher degree of collaboration between them and us for the benefit of all life. I am also deeply grateful to my Lorian colleagues Jeremy Berg and Freya Secrest whose tireless energy and work has made possible all the classes which have been so integral to my own research process and from which this material has evolved. Thanks, too, to my lovely wife Julia whose partnership and love makes all this work possible. Finally, thanks to the hundreds of students and colleagues who have worked with me over the years, testing the exercises, exploring the material, and invoking new insights through excellent questions and sharing experiences of their own concerning the incarnational process. The value that Incarnational Spirituality brings to the world is due to all of you.

Publications by David Spangler

Books

Subtle Worlds: *An Explorer's Field Notes*
Blessing: *The Art and the Practice*
The Call
Parent as Mystic - Mystic as Parent
Everyday Miracles
The Laws of Manifestation
The Story Tree
The Incarnational Card Deck and Manual
The Flame of Incarnation
Apprenticed to Spirit
A Midsummer's Journey with the Sidhe

Lorian Textbook Series

World Work
Crafting Home: *Generating the Sacred*
Space-Crafting: *The Holding of Self*
Crafting Relationships: *The Holding of Others*
Crafting Inner Alliances: *The Holding of Spirit*

Card Decks with Manuals

Manifestation: *Creating the life you love*
The Soul's Oracle
The Card Deck of the Sidhe

Contents

Introduction 1

Chapter One: The Principles Of Incarnation.............................5

    Exercises 16
        Standing Exercise 16
        Holding Exercises: The Lap 17
        Self-Lap 19

Chapter Two: The Generative Self 21

    Exercises...46
        Presence Exercise..46
        Self-Light Exercises 50
        Expanded Self-Light Exercise 50
        Simple Self-Light Exercise....................................51
        When Stars Meet..52
        Exploring The Generative Self...............................52
        The Inner Solar Womb..53
        Your Inner "Chlorophyll" 53

Chapter Three: Earth's Subtle Ecology 55

    Exercises...66
        Going To The Beach 66
        Cleansing Hands (Energy Hygiene)......................68

Chapter Four: Gaia 71

    Exercises...78
        Grail Space..78
        Earth Core, Life Light 80

Chapter Five: Working With The Subtle Half 83

    Exercises 98
        Basic Energy Hygiene Exercise 98
        Energy Hygiene Using Grail Space 99
        Subtle Activism: The Basic Process With Example..........101
        Massaging The World: A Subtle Activism Exercise 104
        Webmaking: A Subtle Activism Exercise 106
        Collaborative Mind 111

Chapter Six: Practicing Incarnational Spirituality..........................115

    Exercises For Chapter Six 120
        The Four Practices 120
        The Four Blessings...121

Next Steps..123

Introduction

This book is an introduction to an incarnational spirituality.
We live in challenging and changing times that are unprecedented in human history. Our spiritual insights and practices need to help us respond appropriately. For centuries much of spirituality has been oriented to transcendental and transpersonal realms and experiences; in some cases, the physical world—and our physical selves—have even been seen as obstructions to discovering and expressing our true natures which were deemed to be not of this earth. While there is much of value to be found in transpersonal, mystical and transcendental experiences, the challenge of our time is to be a harmonious and collaborative part of the earth. We are asked to be more present to the physical world, not less. Environmental degradation, climate change, the increase in pollution, and the diminishment of fossil fuels and other invaluable resources with the consequent rising cost of energy to power our civilization are not mystical or abstract challenges. They are concrete problems rising from how we relate to the physical world around us, to each other, and to ourselves. They are incarnational problems.

Yet the solutions to them are not entirely physical. In addition to their material causes, these challenges come from attitudes and beliefs we hold, some of them very ancient and rooted in religious and spiritual ways of thinking. To meet the needs of our time, we need to reexamine these beliefs and attitudes. We must develop a deeper and more holistic form of spirituality in order to do so. We need spiritual perspectives that enable us to connect to the world more skillfully, intimately and collaboratively. We need a spirituality that helps us incarnate more fully to meet the incarnational problems of the planet.

This book is an introduction to just such a spirituality. In offering it, I do not claim that it is the only way or that it holds all the answers. It is one contribution among many to a planetary project in which humanity is engaged. This project is no less than an effort to develop new ways of understanding and expressing ourselves in relationship to our planetary home so that we can create a world of grace and blessing, compassion and safety for all.

Incarnation is more than simply being on earth in a body. It is a collaborative partnership between our incarnating consciousnesses and the environments in which our incarnations are taking place. Aside from whatever else it offers or makes possible, this partnership is a creative process that does three things. It connects and engages with the environment, it fosters emergence and the development of potentials within the incarnating consciousness and the environment, and it promotes wholeness. In my words, incarnation is a holopoietic process, that is, one that produces wholeness, integration, and coherency.

Our bodies know how to do these three things: connect, develop, and create wholeness. When they fail to do so for some reason, we fall ill and may die. But at the macro level of society and our collective interactions with each other and with the natural world around us, we struggle to implement these three basic aspects of incarnation. We have yet to create a society that fosters creativity and learning, one that creates integration and wholeness between all its members and between itself and the larger world, or one that fosters the emergence of the potentials of consciousness and spirit within the world. The problem is not that humanity is too incarnated and needs to be more transcendental and "spiritual;" the problem is that we're not incarnated enough. We all have an incarnational intelligence that inherently knows how to be here on earth in a body; our challenge is—and has been—knowing how to embody that intelligence in our daily lives and to extend its principles and operations into the larger domain of society and environmental responsibility. Understanding that intelligence and how to express it is what Incarnational Spirituality is all about.

Right now most of humanity is either in or is affected by a technological society that gives us great power to do things in the world but not necessarily the wisdom or insights—or the holopoietic knowledge—to do them in a holistic or incarnational manner.

The result is the spectrum of global problems that are facing us; along with them comes the fundamental challenge—and opportunity—of our historical moment. This is to learn to live in wholeness and harmony with our world and with ourselves. We need to become ecologically and socially wise in ways that have not yet been achieved at a planetary level in human history. We truly need to learn how to incarnate skillfully on this planet and with each other.

This is why I believe that incarnational spirituality and the insights and practices it offers are an important contribution at this time.

Embodying an incarnational intelligence, you possess inner resources that can lead to a more empowered, holistic, and integrated way of being, one that can be a blessing to you and to the world in which you live. This is the promise of Incarnational Spirituality and the incarnational way.

This book is an introduction to this promise. If it stimulates your interest and you'd like to go further, then at the end of the book are suggestions for next steps you can take to pursue this study and gain deeper insights into Incarnational Spirituality and the skills it offers.

The Exercises

In our Lorian classes and programs, much of our practical work revolves around doing exercises. I include a number of these exercises in this book. Some of them are simple mini-rituals; others are more reflective or contemplative. Some are intended to stimulate a particular kind of energy field around or within you, or connect you energetically with the world in a specific way. All are concerned with creating a state of mind, a felt sense, within you.

These exercises are just suggestions. They are not cast in concrete. If you understand the purpose of the exercise, then you can feel free to redesign it and adapt it to your particular style and needs. Indeed, I encourage you to do so, so that you can make the exercise your own.

An exercise is a living thing, filled with spirit, and it should blend with you in a way that honors and fosters your own spirit. In doing the exercise, it should emerge from you as much as from

3

me and transform itself in any way that is needful in order for that to happen. It may contain elements that you may not wish to do or that seem too elaborate or just not your "style." All I ask is that you understand and honor the purpose behind the exercise, the spirit it is intended to embody or the felt sense within you that it's designed to foster. Then feel free to change it or adapt it as you need. To paraphrase Jesus, you were not made for the exercises. The exercises are made to serve you.

Try each exercise once as presented, but please feel free after that to modify the form of the exercise if you wish to configure it to your unique needs and style. In so doing, however, be sure to retain the integrity of the basic objective and intent.

If at any time in doing an exercise, you feel discomfort of any kind, tiredness, restlessness, or a sense that something is amiss, then stop doing it. This doesn't necessarily mean that you've come into contact with something dangerous or harmful, only that for some reason your energy in the moment is flagging or is no longer compatible with what you're doing. Change your attention completely. Do something physical to shift and change your energy. Do something fun that makes you laugh, which is also an excellent way to change your energy.

If in doing an exercise, you get an inner "No!" about it, then please stop doing it. It may be a matter of timing, it may be that you are tired, or it may be that this exercise is not for you. As I said above, make the exercise your own. If need be, adjust it so you feel comfortable with it, or find a substitute.

Remember, if this happens, it may only be a matter of timing or that you are tired. Unless you have a strong inner sense not to do so, I would recommend trying the exercise one more time later. If the sense of disturbance or uneasiness continues, then definitely this exercise is not for you. Either change it or find some equivalent or simply skip it entirely.

In doing inner work of this nature, the rule "No Pain, No Gain" most definitely does NOT apply!

Chapter One: The Principles of Incarnation

Incarnation is not simply a matter of a soul stepping into and taking over a physical body the way a driver might enter a car. It's a complex and continuous collaborative and integrative process involving both physical and non-physical elements. This whole process is orchestrated by an "incarnational intelligence," an inner knowing of how to make this process work. We all have this incarnational intelligence within us—we couldn't incarnate at all without it—but its operations are mainly unconscious, much like the intelligent processes that run our bodies usually do so without our conscious knowledge. However, this incarnational intelligence becomes accessible to our everyday awareness when we act in accordance with its underlying principles. I can choose to mindfully express the basic principles of incarnation in my activities, and when I do, I begin to consciously align with and express this deeper incarnational intelligence, making it a practical part of my life.

The five basic principles of incarnation that help form this incarnational intelligence are:

1. The Principle of Identity, which manifests intent.
2. The Principle of Boundary which manifests holding.
3. The Principle of Connection and Engagement which manifests relationship.
4. The Principle of Emergence which manifests newness, learning and discovery.
5. The Principle of Holopoiesis which manifests integration, coherency and wholeness.

Incarnation occurs when something takes shape and substance and forms connections within a particular environment. In any such process we can see each of these principles at work. This is true whether it's the incarnation of something as simple as a meal or as complex as a person or a business, or even a nation. The skillful application and expression of these principles leads to a successful incarnation.

Identity

Incarnation begins with identity. Something is incarnating. That something is determined by its identity. This identity might also be expressed as an intention. For instance, the Ford Motor Company began as an intention to manufacture and sell automobiles; this intent gave it the identity of being an automotive corporation. My life began as an intention of my soul to be a participant in the physical life of the earth and the collective life of humanity. This intent gives me the identity of being a human being.

Locating the original intent is not always simple. We could say that Ford Motors grew out of Henry Ford's desire to be an inventor, for example, or is a particular manifestation of his overall incarnation as a businessperson. In describing how my Christmas stories "incarnate," I said that their original identity could be seen as gifts which then took the form of stories rather than that of paintings or sculptures.

In a similar way, it's been my observation that the original intent and identity behind our human incarnations isn't necessarily to fulfill a particular task or goal, such as being a doctor, working out some kind of karma, or becoming President of the United States. Our incarnations—perhaps even all incarnations for all beings—ultimately arise out of love and a desire to be of service to the world as a whole. This intent may not in the end be strong or clear enough to manifest in our individual lives, but it's there within the soul nonetheless. In this sense, I could say that our core incarnational identity is love.

Boundary

Boundaries create distinctions. They tell where something begins and where it ends. They give concrete expression to an identity, establishing the difference between what is "I" and what is "not-I." They separate one thing from another.

A boundary need not be a barrier or a wall; it can be a threshold, a membrane, a function, or an activity. For example, being able to swim would be a boundary between those who are on a swim team and those who aren't.

Spiritual teachings often stress the need to overcome separation and experience oneness. There is certainly value in this. The underlying spirit of all life does indeed unite us. But incarnational spirituality distinguishes between separation and divisiveness. Separation is not necessarily a negative state. It creates the conditions that allow individuality and uniqueness to develop and these in turn spark the engine of creativity.

We can see this expressed in the old adage that two heads are better than one. This acknowledges that bringing together two minds that are different—that are separated from each other—allows each to bring its own unique perspectives and thus enhance a creative process. Together they can see more than either might do on its own.

Here's another example of the importance of individuality. Take an ordinary sheet of paper such as you might use in a computer printer and take an equal sized sheet of paper toweling. Spill some water on a table and then use each sheet to clean it up. Which one absorbs more water? I've done this experiment to illustrate this point, and it's always the paper towel that is more absorbent. Why is this so? Because it has greater surface area than ordinary printer paper, even when they are both the same dimensions in size. The reason is the paper towel is covered with hundreds of small bumps and ridges. Such convolutions are what increase the surface area of your intestines and your brain as well. This is important because the surface is where interaction takes place: where water (or food) is absorbed, where nerve connections are made and so forth.

When there is one person, the creative "surface area" (all things being equal) is one, let's say. But when there are two people, this creative surface area isn't just doubled. It expands exponentially. Where creativity is concerned, one plus one doesn't necessarily equal two. It can equal three as something new emerges that expands the potential of the two minds working together.

But none of this would be possible without boundaries, without a principle that separates one thing from another so that the "surface area" is increased. The "bumps" and ridges on a paper towel are separated from each other on the surface of the paper sheet, thereby increasing the amount of that surface that can be used to absorb spilled liquids.

Boundaries create diversity. They enable one huge, super, cosmic "I" to become a multitude of individual "I's" each offering its own unique contribution to a larger wholeness and thus enriching the creative potential of the community of life.

This is not the only function of boundaries, however. If a boundary connects with itself, it creates an outside and an inside. That "inside" is where something can be held. As I sit here writing, my coffee cup is on my desk. The boundary of the cup creates a space that can contain and hold my hot coffee, preventing it from spilling over everything. The boundary turns space into a container.

My coffee cup is a passive holder. By itself, it doesn't affect whatever is poured into it. But a cell membrane is not passive. It is an active participant, regulating or affecting both the internal processes of the cell and its relationships with its environment. The cell wall is a living, permeable, interactive boundary, and through its activity it has the capacity to change what happens in the cell interior. It holds the life of the cell in a participatory way.

Incarnation depends on the principle of holding. Your life and consciousness are held in a physical body that is separated by the boundary of your skin from the environment. They are also held in subtle fields of energy that enable your individual thoughts and feelings to develop in unique ways that give your personality its unique nature. These subtle fields are energetic boundaries invisible to the eye but acting as inner "skins" within the non-physical environment. They differentiate you from all other beings and create a space within which your individual capacities and potentials may develop.

Boundary creates the space within which the foundational elements—the "DNA"—of the incarnation are gathered and held and within which they interact to bring the specific characteristics of this life into being.

Connection and Engagement

Boundaries create spaces that are distinct, contained and unique. Without the ability to connect, these spaces can become isolated. Boundaries manifest the positive aspects of separation, but connection opens the door to engagement and relationship and prevents that separation from turning into divisiveness and alienation.

The incarnational process might be seen as a play. Identity and boundary make it possible for the actor to assume a distinct role and show up on stage—they are necessary to be embodied. But embodiment is not sufficient. Appearing on stage is only the first step. At that point the actor needs to connect to the other actors, to the setting, and to the audience and engage them. It's through their interaction that the play unfolds and people leave the theater feeling satisfied.

Boundary and Identity establish the Why and Who of an incarnation. Connection enables the relationships and interactions that establish the What, Where, and When. Out of engagement with our environment, our parents, our friends, our culture, and the natural world that enfolds all of us, we develop the specific content of our lives. Connections are the vocabulary from which our autobiographies are written.

The relationships we form with people at a conscious level are only a small part of the whole spectrum of connectedness that characterizes our lives and makes incarnation possible. We are connected to the world at cellular and molecular levels in ways we hardly ever think about or suspect, unless we get sick from a virus or bacteria.

There are connections that we are born into, such as the blood ties with parents and siblings, or on a planetary scale, the metabolic ties we share with all carbon-based forms of life. But most connections we need to form. This is true even with those with whom we are automatically related in some manner. My children are blood kin but that doesn't mean that we are connected in psychological and social ways. I need to create those connections through love and communication, doing things together and sharing my individuality with theirs. But there are already bonds there with my kids that facilitate these more extensive connections. This is not the case with nearly everyone else I meet. I need to discover the ways in which my unique identity can connect with theirs. This process of forming connections is the meat of incarnation.

Incarnation literally means to "take on flesh." Relationships and engagement form the substance of that flesh.

Emergence

There is nothing linear about incarnation. It's not like a machine in which you put in some materials and out comes a widget. It's not a closed system. Imagine a machine that interacts with its environment in such a way that when you put in raw materials, a widget might come out but you could not predict its color or texture, or for that matter whether it would even be a widget; it could be a wodget or a wadget or even a tegdiw (that's a reverse widget). What is produced emerges from the interaction of raw materials, the machine, and the environment. While the end result is roughly predictable, it's not entirely so.

Emergent properties are a vital part of nature. Take two poisons, sodium and chloride, and put them together. By all reasoning, one would expect another poison but instead you get salt, which is essential to life. Or even more basically, who would predict the qualities of water such as wetness and flow from an analysis of the two elements, both gases, from which it comes, hydrogen and oxygen? These qualities are emergent. They are a surprise, as if you'd put a "wid" and a "get" together and got a floozle instead of a widget.

You and I are emergent beings. There are those who say that the soul plans everything out in advance, that our lives are simply the outworking of a plan already known and established in the heavens. But this is not true. Nor would we—or our souls—want it to be true.

Think about it. We create our designs—whether it's the design of a widget or the design of a life—based on what we already know, not on what we don't know or can't know yet. If I know that without question or exception my machine will take raw materials and make widgets, then there is no discovery here, only known and predictable consequences. In effect, it's no more than the past made visible. Of course we need this predictability and structure in our lives, too, but our lives as a whole operate on a different principle, one of discovery, growth, learning, innovation, creativity—in short on a principle of emergence.

Emergence manifests in our lives in a variety of ways. Usually we call it learning or growth. We start out heading towards A and twenty years later we are in B. This certainly happened to me. I entered college fully convinced I would be a molecular biologist. I had my eyes firmly fixed on doing cellular research, perhaps in the field of genetics, and in my deepest, wildest fantasies, I imagined myself in Stockholm receiving a Nobel Prize in chemistry or biology for having discovered something fundamental about how we come to be who we are. But three years later, I had left school and was standing alone on a stage in Los Angeles, giving a talk on spirituality and taking the first steps to becoming a spiritual teacher. Who would have guessed? My work emerged and it took me in directions I didn't predict.

Holopoiesis

Putting these four principles together, though, doesn't guarantee integration or coherency. All four principles are at work in us, but each of us certainly has had experiences of feeling a lack of integration or coherency in our lives. Disease results when this incoherency manifests on a physical level, and conflict arises when it manifests in the realm of our relationships.

This is where the fifth principle comes in. It's the glue that holds the other four together and allows them to work as a whole system. I call it holopoiesis (pronounced ho-lo-po-ee-sis) from the Greek holo- for "whole" and –poiesis for "production." Thus it means "the production of wholes" or "the creation of wholeness."

Holopoiesis is an impulse running through all creation to achieve wholeness and to participate in the creation of larger wholes;

it's a self-organizing principle that can lead to more integrated, connected and complex systems. Simply becoming more complex or larger is insufficient if the various participating and contributing elements cannot integrate and work together coherently.

From a spiritual standpoint, the most obvious expression of holopoiesis is love. Or perhaps I should say that love is the operating methodology of holopoiesis, the means by which wholes are brought into being with integration and coherency. However, love is not the only means by which holopoiesis operates. Intentionality plays a key role as well manifesting as a will to build connections and create wholeness in any given situation.

An Incarnational Intelligence

When I sit down to write a story, I know how to blend the ingredients of vocabulary, grammar, syntax, plot, characterization, setting, and so forth into the tale I wish to create. I have the knowledge of how to do so. (Whether I have the skill to write well is another matter!) I have what might be called a "writer's intelligence." Similarly, my body does all kinds of things—it digests food, takes in oxygen, passes messages along nerve channels, heals cuts, fights germs—that keep me alive and healthy. It knows how to do these things; it has the knowledge of embodiment. I could call that my "body intelligence."

Likewise, there is part of us that knows how to incarnate. It knows how to apply the five principles (and perhaps others that I haven't yet discovered or named) to manifest the coherent and integrated system that is an individual life. This is what I call the "incarnational intelligence." Fundamentally, I feel this intelligence is part of our souls; after all, it is the soul that is incarnating. But it is also part of our everyday lives, part of what we do. We are not being incarnated in some passive way; we are incarnating in a very active sense.

Learning how to skillfully express this incarnational intelligence is a powerful way to make our life—our incarnation—a blessing to ourselves and to the world around us. Given that everything—the world, humanity, the creatures of nature, other people, and even the sacred itself—is incarnating, the more that we can mindfully attune to and align with this intelligence and its five principles, the more we are in alignment and attunement with everything around us. It is a way of integrating with the spiritual forces behind the manifestation of the world.

That's why I think of this approach as an incarnational spirituality and incarnation itself as a spiritual practice. When we practice expressing an incarnational intelligence, we are practicing our own life and our own spirit, and we are practicing the life and spirit of the world.

Applying the Principles

These five principles are meant to be lived, not simply described. In fact, we can't avoid living them out. Every day we are dealing with identities—our own and those of the people around us, not to mention the identities of the creatures and things that make up our environment—boundaries, connections and relationships, and emergence. We are all seeking to create wholeness and to be more integrated and coherent—or at least to avoid dis-integration and incoherency. Failure to apply one or more of these principles skillfully and successfully invariably leads to problems.

For example, there have been times when I've been asked to consult with groups that are having difficulties organizationally. I often find that the core problem is a lack of clear identity. Often too many people are trying to determine just what kind of organization it is and what it should be doing, and no one is synthesizing these ideas into a shared direction. A lack of clear identity can then lead to a lack of clear boundaries, and this in turn can lead to failed or missed connections or making the wrong connections. What emerges from all this is a crippled organization, one that is not living up to its potentials and definitely not being as coherent and integrated as it could be.

I am not a counselor, but occasionally people come to me as a teacher to discuss life problems. Often I discover that the basic problem is a lack of clear boundaries. The individual is too susceptible to the opinions and directions of others, or is too open to subtle energies, and this creates a challenge to maintaining their own identity and integration.

The Incarnational intelligence is aware that it is incarnating through its actions and application of the principles. It knows that incarnation is a process, an activity, and not a one-time event that happened just when we were born.

Practicing an incarnational intelligence means being mindful of what I am doing that's shaping my life. It's an awareness of incarnation as an ongoing, continuous, participatory, unfolding process.

This is deeper than just a situational awareness, however, or mindfulness of my actions. It's also an honoring and an appreciation of the fact of incarnation and the privilege it offers to be part of this world. Humanity's great spiritual traditions all honor the earth and the value of human life. Yet there are attitudes within these traditions that turn our attention exclusively towards transcendental levels of being and that view the spiritual worlds with longing, despising and deprecating physical existence. An incarnational awareness rejects such attitudes without rejecting the transcendent per se. It acknowledges the value of being here on earth, even if at times it can be challenging and painful. It understands that to participate in the act of incarnation is to participate in a most fundamental sacred act, for the principles of incarnation may be understood as principles undergirding the existence and growth of all creation. The universe is God's incarnation. The root of incarnational intelligence—indeed, the Primal Incarnational Intelligence itself which is present in all of us—is firmly within the generative mystery that is the Sacred.

In honoring your incarnation, you pay attention to how you are embodying and expressing the five principles in your life. What is your identity? How do you express yourself? What are your boundaries like? What do you accept or reject; what do you let in and what do you keep out? What connections and relationships are you forming with your world? How are you engaged? What are you learning? How are you growing? How coherent is your life? How do you create wholeness around yourself? Questions like these help you be aware of the activity of these five principles in your life; they help you to be mindful of your incarnational process.

When we are mindful in this way, it gives us a new way of seeing ourselves, a new sense of personal identity and power. And it opens the door to discovering and expressing our generative selves and tapping the resource of our own Self-Light.

EXERCISES FOR CHAPTER ONE

STANDING EXERCISE

This is a core exercise in the practice of Incarnational Spirituality. It is a way of attuning to Identity and Sovereignty (more about this in the next chapter) and to the uniqueness, strength and presence of one's individuality. In doing this exercise of Standing, physically stand if you are able. If you are not able to do so, then be as upright as you can be in your physical situation and "stand" mentally and emotionally. As you do so, work through these levels of sensation, feeling, thought, energy, and spirit, appreciating the power, the freedom, the sovereignty, and the presence emerging within you from the simple act of standing.

Physical:
The physical action of this exercise is simple. From a sitting position, you simply stand up. Be aware of the physical sensation and felt sense of standing. Feel the work of your body, the power of balance that keeps you upright. If you are already standing, become aware that you are standing and be mindful of the felt sense of standing. In standing you are asserting your physical power to rise up against the power of gravity that would pull you down. You are celebrating your strength. If you are physically unable to stand, you can still assume an inner attitude of standing, perhaps simply by straightening your spine as much as possible.

Emotional:
Feel the power of being upright. Feel how standing singles you out and expresses your individuality. You stand for what you believe, you stand up to be counted. Standing proclaims that you are here. Standing says you are ready to make choices and decisions. Feel the strength and presence of your identity and sovereignty.

Mental:
Celebrate your humanness. You are an upright being. You

emerge from the mass of nature, from the vegetative and animal states into a realm of thinking and imagining. In standing, you hands are released from providing locomotion. Feel the freedom of your hands that don't have to support you but can now be used to create, manipulate, touch, and express your thoughts and imagination.

Magical (Energetic):

When you stand, your spine becomes a magical staff, the axis mundi and center of your personal world, generating the field that embraces you. The spine is the traditional wizard's staff along which dragon power flows and the centers of energy sing in resonance with the cosmos. Feel your energy field coming into alignment with the stars above, the earth below, and the environment around you.

Spiritual:

Standing, you are the incarnate link between heaven and earth. Your energy rises into the sky and descends into the earth. Light descends and ascends, swirling along your spine in a marriage of matter and spirit. This energy is both personal and transpersonal, giving birth to something new, something human, individual and unique. Feel the magic and energy of your sovereignty that connects soul to person, the higher-order consciousness with the consciousness of the incarnate realms. Feel the will that emerges from this connection, the spiritual presence that blends heaven and earth.

HOLDING EXERCISES

Holding is a result of having boundaries that create a space that can contain something else. In this exercise, the boundaries are established by your own body as you sit to create a lap.

The Lap

This exercise is very simple: sitting down and forming a lap. A lap is a physical form of holding. When we sit, our bodies form a kind of bowl or cup. Imagine kids climbing into a lap: it is a place of love, comfort, healing, and transformation. Imagine when you climbed into a lap and how good and safe it felt. In this exercise, simply sit down and form a lap. Go through the following elements as you do so, exploring the felt sense of each. Inherent in the lap is your power to create a boundary and to hold.

Physical:

The physical action of this exercise is simplicity itself. From a standing position, you simply sit down, allowing your legs to form a lap. Be aware of the physical sensation and felt sense of being a lap. Feel the relaxation of sitting but at the same time the power and receptivity of forming a lap. Explore the felt sense of the space that is created in front of you, around you, and within you when you sit and form a lap.

Emotional:

Feel the power of being a space of holding. In your lap, you are forming a space of comfort, a space of healing, a space of encouragement and upliftment. In this space, negativity can be received and transformed as you hold a presence of peace, of love, and of strength.

Mental:

Your mind is also a lap. It is a cup that holds your thoughts. As you sit, let your mind go beyond the contents of any thoughts you may be holding. Let it simply appreciate the power of holding thoughts. Appreciate your mental space, the spaciousness of your mind. If thoughts come within this space, simply welcome them and let them sit in your mind-lap for a time, then move on. Remember, you are holding them, they are not holding you. You create and own the space they occupy. Sit in that space, be at peace, and feel the power of your mind to be a lap.

"Magical" (Energetic):

The cup is the oldest of magical images. It is the grail of the sacred, the cauldron of magic and wisdom, the cooking pot that creates nourishment, the womb of life, the cup that holds the cosmos. Your lap is this space, this grail, this cauldron, this womb, and this cup. When you sit and a lap is formed, you are in resonance with this primal container and its spaciousness—the womb of God from which new life is born.

Spiritual:
Sitting, your lap is the presence of the sacred. It is a place of love, a place to receive and comfort pain and suffering, a place of healing, a place of rebirth and regeneration. In the space of your lap you are in resonance with the sacred space that holds all things and allows them to be. God is a lap!

Self-Lap

This exercise is a variant expression of the Lap exercise in which you are holding your self.

Step One:
Do the Standing Exercise, feeling your own sovereignty and the power of your individuality.

Step Two:
Draw that power into yourself and do the Lap Exercise, creating a lap both physically and inwardly as a state of mind and being. Let yourself enter a condition of holding empowered by your sovereignty and individuality.

Step Three:
Place yourself in your "lap." Hold yourself. Gather all the parts of you that you can think of, including those parts that you may not like so much or feel cause you problems. You are not doing anything to these parts or selves; you are just holding. In so doing, gain a felt sense of the will that holds you together, so to speak. There is in each of us that which is willing to be incarnate, willing to have parts, willing to have a personality, willing to have a body, willing

19

to create a space that holds all the elements of our lives. How do you experience that? What is the felt sense of it to you? What is the love that holds you?

Step Four:
Just let yourself be held and honored by yourself, by your own inner lap.

Step Five:
When you feel this is complete, just stand up and let your lap dissolve. But remember that you continue to hold yourself. As you go through your day, encountering things in your environment that would snag and pull you apart or things in yourself that would divide you and pull you apart, remember the will that holds. Remember your lap. Remember to hold yourself again in love.

Chapter Two: The Generative Self

The Self

Incarnational Spirituality honors who we are as unique incarnate individuals and seeks to enable us to express the creativity and energy inherent both in the incarnational process and in the phenomenon of selfhood. There are some spiritual traditions that view the self as an eternal reality—Christianity is one of these—and there are other spiritual traditions, most notably in the East, that view the self as non-existent and an illusion. My own experiences working with the subtle worlds lead me to a viewpoint that lies between these two. The Self is not a thing that we possess in the way that we might possess a car or a house, but it's not purely a fiction either, like a dream that will evaporate upon awakening. The self has a real existence and effect in the world. It is a presence that is constantly emerging and manifesting from a stable process governed by the interaction of the five principles of incarnation we explored in the last chapter. It is the expression of an identity, the manifestation of a set of boundaries, a means of connection and engagement with the world, an emergent phenomenon, and perhaps above all, a means by which wholeness may be introduced and enhanced within the world.

Incarnational Spirituality sees the self as the "grail" that can hold the presence of the soul and bring a spirit of wholeness into the world. Whatever the ultimate nature of the self, its function is to hold consciousness and life, enabling them to participate in the shaping of the world. As such, the self has three key elements. I call them sovereignty, self-light and generativity. In this chapter we are going to look at each of these three.

The Incarnational Challenge

Before we get to these three elements, however, I need to provide some background and context. Keep in mind that this is just an introductory text; my objective here is to outline the territory of Incarnational Spirituality without going too deeply into it. That deeper exploration can be found elsewhere in other texts and books and in the classes and self-study modules that Lorian offers. Still, to fully explain what I mean by sovereignty, self-light and generativity, we need to dip our toes into some esoteric and mystical waters. I'd like you to note that the material that follows is based on my personal intuitive and clairvoyant research in cooperation with non-physical colleagues and as such represents one person's perspective.

But first, let me tell a story from the history of physics.

For centuries, people have known of the three states of matter: solid, liquid and gas. But in 1879, Sir William Crookes, working in his private laboratory in London with early vacuum tubes, identified what came to be known as a fourth state. He named the gas-like phenomenon he observed "radiant matter" because of the way it glowed, but modern science calls it plasma. As it turned out, plasma was found to be the most common form of matter in the universe because all stars are made of it. We see plasma at work when we look at the glowing mass of our sun.

Plasmas exist over an extremely wide range of temperatures, including those one would find at the core of the sun. This created a problem. Scientists wanted to investigate such plasmas, but they were so hot that no physical container could hold them without vaporizing. The challenge was how to contain such plasmas so they could be studied.

The answer was that these very hot plasmas had to be held by something that was insubstantial, something that could not melt. This turned out to be a "magnetic bottle," a field phenomenon created by the interaction of specially designed magnets. The field these magnets generated between them created the boundaries that could contain the plasmas.

The magnetic bottle that can contain super-hot plasmas isn't a "thing." It's a dynamic magnetic process emerging from a set of relationships. It has no substance of its own but it's quite real and substantial nonetheless due to the relationships that enable it to remain in existence. The plasma is contained in a field of relationships.

There is an incarnational challenge that is metaphorically similar to the challenge the scientists faced in trying to hold and contain very hot plasmas. This challenge can be stated thusly: how can a multi-dimensional consciousness and life form become part of a three-dimensional world? How can a wave become part of a world of particles?

Put in more spiritual terms, how can the soul, a relatively unbounded and multi-dimensional state of being and sentiency, be held in a bounded and three-dimensional body and accompanying subtle energy field appropriate to existence on this earth?

The soul is very much more than simply the non-physical side of our personalities; it is more than just the part of us that survives after physical death. The soul exists in a very high energy state that extends into more dimensions of being than simply the three dimensions we're familiar with. I call it a "Higher Order Being." By comparison to the physical, incarnate world, the soul—your soul, my soul, and the souls of all beings—is "hot." Metaphorically, it's like plasma.

The answer to this incarnational challenge is analogous to the answer to the plasma problem. The part of the soul that incarnates is held in a field, a kind of "incarnational bottle" that is in principle akin to a magnetic bottle in that it is a container generated by relationships. (If you would like a further discussion of this incarnational challenge and the soul's approach to it, I recommend an audio CD of a lecture I gave called "Being Particular;" it is available from the Bookstore on the Lorian website.)

The Incarnational System

It is a common and logical assumption that we incarnate into a body. In fact, we incarnate into a complex interactive field, an "incarnational system." This incarnational field—the "magnetic bottle" for our soul—includes our body but is not limited to it. Indeed, our physical body itself exists within this field and is nourished and influenced by it.

Incarnation itself is a relationship between two distinct orders of life and consciousness, one that is multi-dimensional and one that is three-dimensional. For this relationship to be possible, it draws on a number of other relationships, the combined effect of which is to generate a holding field within which the soul can manifest as an emerging and unfolding Self.

These other relationships include co-creative interactions between the soul and the energy field of the planet itself, between the soul and the collective field of humanity, between the soul and the forces and powers of nature (which hold and express the principles and laws of physics, chemistry and biology), and between the soul and various subtle forces and energies. Then there are the specific physical relationships that make embodiment possible, such as the sexual union of a man and a woman who become the father and mother of the incoming soul. Add to this all the other formative relationships we form with siblings, friends, teachers, the land where we dwell and the culture we dwell in. Then add the various relationships between the living cells that make up our bodies and the tissues and organs which they create and which express our human structure and metabolism. You can see how complex the web is of interconnections and interactions that make incarnation possible. This web is our incarnational system.

Of course, we experience ourselves as a singular identity whom we call "myself" or "I." We're certainly aware of many of our various relationships and how they affect us, but we probably don't think of ourselves as "plasma beings" held by a "magnetic bottle" of incarnational interactions, much less as a collection of interacting systems creating such a "bottle." Still, there are some advantages to looking at ourselves through a systemic and relational lens.

The Relationship of Soul and Personality

In the early Seventies I lived in Scotland as a co-director of the Findhorn Foundation community. My fellow co-director was one of the three founders of this center, Peter Caddy, and he came out of a spiritual background that emphasized the overcoming of the personality. For Peter, our human problems were created by our personalities. Certainly in the community, when things would go wrong, invariably he would say that someone had been acting from "the personality level." The spiritual path for him was one of overcoming and subjugating the personality to the rule of the soul and of the Sacred.

This is by no means an unusual perspective. A number of spiritual and esoteric traditions view the personality as the "joker in the deck," the "lower self" or even the "false self" that obstructs the will and flow of spirit and consequently gets us and the world into trouble. The prescription is to get rid of or dominate this flawed, fallen or lesser part of ourselves in order that our "true" self may manifest.

There is obviously truth to the fact that we can act with limited perspectives and in ways that create harm, suffering, violence, and negativity. We have all felt the way in which our personal self, our personality, can feel incoherent, nasty, small-minded, petty, and so forth. But is this due to an inherent flaw in the personality? Is this an inherently broken part of us?

We know that for all the negativity we can produce, we can also manifest compassion, love, and blessing. Do these positive qualities only come from some "higher" part of ourselves? Are we doomed to a split between being an angel and a devil, our lives dominated by a continuing conflict between the soul that is the source of goodness and the personality that is the source of evil?

Not that we don't have to curb some tendencies and enhance others or learn how to behave and act in the world with grace and kindness. Rather it's the image of ourselves as being innately divided into a good side and a bad side, a true side and a false side, which is the problem, for this perspective cannot help but commit us to ongoing conflict. And this inner conflict becomes projected out to become actual conflicts in the world. Consider as well how much mental and emotional energy we spend waging this inner battle, energy that could be spent in creative visioning and activity. We carry burdens of shame, guilt, rage, and a lack of trust in ourselves; how can we build a positive future on such a foundation? How can we face the future when at times it's hard to even face ourselves?

This is where the systemic view of incarnation can be helpful. It changes the image of our selves from that of two combating contestants facing off in a ring, each trying to knock the other out to that of a group of athletes, each with different skills and capacities, trying to work together and form an integrated team. When things go wrong, the fault doesn't fall on one member of the team alone. It is seen as a lack of integration and coherency; the system as a whole isn't working right and all the members share the responsibility for this.

Soul and personality are in partnership and collaboration; indeed, they are really two sides of the same identity. They are part of a single system that is seeking coherency, integration and wholeness. Our objective is not to overcome, ignore or get rid of one or the other of these partners. Our objective is to enable the system as a whole to function in wholeness—to get the partners collaborating properly, to use one metaphor, or to get the team functioning as an integrated whole, to use another.

Team Self

If I use the metaphor of a team effort to describe the emergence of the incarnate self, just who or what are the members of this team? Of course, as a metaphor the composition of "Team Self" could be described in a number of different ways; the important point is that incarnation is a collaborative effort, however we name or number the elements that contribute to that collaboration. For example, here is one way the members of Team Self can be described:

- The Soul: This represents the transpersonal part of ourselves, our high self, inner divinity, the non-physical or spiritual side of our nature, and so on. This is our sacredness.
- The Everyday Self or Personality: This is our incarnate individuality, the part of us we usually think of when we think of our identity or who we are.
- The "World Self:" This is the part of us that is connected to the substances and processes of the physical world, to the forces of Nature and the biosphere, to "Gaia" or the soul of the world. This is our "naturalness."

- The "Human Self:" This is the part of us that is connected to humanity and human nature as a whole, to the Soul of Humanity, and to the historical moment and destiny through which humanity is living and evolving. This is our humanness.

In effect, to incarnate, the soul must make contact with and form connections with the living field of the earth and with the energies of nature and the biosphere in order to fashion a physical body, and it must make contact and connection with the collective mental, emotional, cultural, and temporal field of humanity as it is manifesting on the earth in order to fashion a particular human self that is at home in the human world. In forming the fields that will hold its incarnating energies, the soul must draw on subtle energies within the natural world and subtle energies within the human world to make sure that its incarnate manifestation is at home in these environments. These are the "magnets" that help create the field that will hold the "plasma" of the soul. Exploring these subtle energetic processes of incarnation is part of the cosmology of Incarnational Spirituality.

Each of the four participants I described above as being part of Team Self or part of Incarnation INC is a unique function in its own right and makes a unique contribution to making us who we are. How does this play out within the individual?

The "Human Self" connects us to other human beings. It is the conduit through which we take on habits, images, ideas, motivations, and so on that come from other people in particular and from human society, history and culture in general. The "Human Self" within us—the humanness within us—is what holds and connects us to cultural worldviews, traditions, and social habits and mores. It contains the mental and emotional images of life that we pick up from parents, siblings, relative, friends, teachers, media, and so on. And it contributes the motivations that come from such images. This is a force within us; it is the source of impulses and energies that arise not from our individuality but from the collective. This is not necessarily a bad thing; in fact, it's a necessary thing if we are to be connected with the rest of humanity. But if it rules the incarnational system, then we end up expressing the collective will and not the will of our individual personhood, or the will of our soul or of the earth.

The "World Self" within us is the part of us that connects to the biological imperatives of nature and the land. It is Gaia, the soul of the world, within us. We most feel its effects through our physical instincts and our sense of belonging to nature. A shaman for whom everything, including clouds, rivers, mountains, and stones, is alive and who is deeply sensitive to the sentiency within nature is in touch with his or her "World Self." By contrast, a modern person surrounded by technology and artificial environments is ignorant of and largely cut off from this part of himself or herself. This is true even if we acknowledge that human-made environments like our cities and the electronic gadgets that fill them are also alive and filled with spirit and are a hybrid of the interaction of Gaia and Humanity. It's not these gadgets or environments in themselves that innately cut us off from the world; rather it's that we have lost the sense of attunement to our own inner "World Self," the presence and life of Gaia within us.

The "Human Self" and the "World Self" together make up what in psychology is called our subconscious.

Our everyday self, our personality, is the part of us with which most people are most familiar. Usually, it's what we mean when we say "I." From an incarnational standpoint, its function is to give us particularity and individuality that enables the soul to engage with this world. I think of the personality as the function within the whole incarnational system that takes universal or collective energies and impulses and translates them into particularity and specificity. It is the personality's function to be, well, selfish, and to see the world through the lens of the personal identity.

The soul is the part of us that maintains contact with the transpersonal realms and what I call the Higher Order Worlds. In common parlance it is the universal and spiritual part of us, in many ways the diametrical opposite of the personality. In the metaphoric language of quantum physics, the soul is the wave to the personality's particle. In psychological terms, it's the superconscious. I'll write more about this in a later section.

One of the common metaphors for incarnation is that of a car and a driver. The soul is often pictured as a driver and the body or the incarnate self as the car which the soul enters and rides around in. This image conveys a linear relationship between the driver and the car or the soul and the personality and body. The metaphor for what I'm suggesting is that of a team. It could be a sports team or it could be something like a jazz band. One instrument and one musician may establish and hold the melody but then all the other musicians and their instruments riff around it and off from it, creating an emergent and improvisational performance that is greater than the sum of the parts. The melody (the soul and its presence and intent) is always there but it weaves in and out of the other sounds and streams of music, sometimes moving to the fore and sometimes falling behind as the overall arrangement unfolds in creative discovery.

The basketball team driving towards a victory and playing as if the team members were one organism or the jazz musicians jamming together to create a unique piece of music, one that has never existed before and will never exist again, are all demonstrating the nature of the incarnational system. They are also demonstrating two vital elements in the quest for wholeness: integration and coherency.

INCarnation

One of the central tasks in our lives is to keep the INC in incarnation. These letters sum up the holopoietic impulse behind Team Self very nicely: "I 'N' C": Integration aNd Coherency. For any system to function well, it needs to be integrated and coherent with all its component or contributing elements relating and working together well.

This is where a simplistic image of incarnation and the self doesn't help us because it can devolve into polarity and adversity. The usual formulations—soul and personality, "true self" and "false self," higher self and lower self, transpersonal and personal—can easily set up a situation of inner conflict. The result of this is to diminish integration and coherency, the INC.

Perfection is not located in just one partner in this incarnational system. No partner or contributor is perfect or immune to error, not even the soul. Each element might be able to function quite well on its own, but within a system, it has to learn how to be part of the collaborative whole.

Think of a basketball team. One player might be a true superstar, an outstanding athlete, but that doesn't mean he can automatically function well in a team. A team made up of superstars might sound like a dream but it can be a nightmare if each of them tries to play in his own way and they don't know how to blend with each other. The holopoietic skill of creating a team—creating wholeness between a group of people engaged in a shared task—is a skill in its own right that needs to be learned and practiced.

Or think of a jazz band. If the musicians don't listen to each other, then the music they produce will be discordant and unpleasant. Here the fault doesn't necessarily lie with one musician alone but with the team process. Everyone is participating in the problem, and everyone has to participate in the solution. Now it may well be that one musician has a better ear for music and another might be a bit tone deaf, but jazz is not simply one musician playing while everyone else is back up. It's a collaborative and co-created art in which the better skilled help the lesser skilled to be part of the team.

When Systems Break Down

No one seeing the news can doubt that human beings are capable of the most extreme acts of violence and destruction. Our inhumanity towards our fellow human beings fills the pages of history as well as the biographies of countless victims of abuse. Our selfish treatment of the environment now threatens our very survival. Why do we act this way? Why do we do the evil that we do?

This is an age old question. Traditionally, the answer has been to postulate a specific source of evil that acts to corrupt our actions and destroy the wholeness of the world. This source might be seen as a devil, or as evil spirits, or, often, as the "ego," the personality, or the "lower" part of us.

As I've already said, this is not the point of view of Incarnational Spirituality. Rather, evil is a consequence of the breakdown of the incarnational system, a result of a loss of coherency. This breakdown can originate with any of the partners in Team Self, though for different reasons, and the breakdown in one can lead to breakdown in another or ultimately in all the members.

In simplest terms, breakdown occurs when a particular part of us is unable or in some cases unwilling to surrender enough of itself to enable a larger wholeness to emerge. There are different reasons why this may be so. The "World Self" is the source of our ancient animal nature, expressed in our reptilian brain; it is the source of instincts for survival and procreation. One of its jobs is to ensure we stay alive and reproduce. It has other qualities, too. Modern research has shown that cooperation, symbiosis, and even altruism are built into our deepest organic processes; they are as much a part of our animal heritage as sexuality and hunger. But when survival becomes the dominant motive, then the instincts acting in the "World Self" can lead a person to act in selfish, predatory ways.

The "Human Self" is connected to the collective thoughts and feelings of humanity. There is greatness in humanity but there is also suffering, pain, fear, anger, hatred, lust, dominance, and other negative qualities that have been generated and reinforced throughout our history. If these become dominant forces acting through our "Human Self," we can find ourselves taking them on, identifying with them, and acting them out. Likewise, the personality has as a function the establishment and preservation of our unique individuality, but expressed without balance, this may never rise above simple selfishness and egoism.

Even the soul is not immune to breakdown, though in this case it isn't the soul itself that is at fault but its capacity to form an appropriate and balanced link with its incarnate self. Incarnation is a skill, and souls are not equal in that skill any more than everyone is equal in the skill of playing the violin or singing. And if the three other partners—personality, Human Self, and World Self—become out of balance, they can make it more difficult for the soul to make its presence felt and its voice heard.

The point is that Team Self can break down, and individual members of this team can end up expressing crippled and crippling attributes which further diminishes the wholeness of the incarnational enterprise. Rather than becoming a manifestation of holopoiesis, the individual ends up manifesting its opposite and becomes a force for separation and divisiveness in the world.

Co-Incarnates

Each of us is a co-incarnate for each other. We assist in each other's incarnation and in the capacity of "Team Self" to integrate and express its holopoietic impulses most effectively. This is especially true if we are close to each other, such as sharing family ties, but it is true even with the strangers whom we meet. Each encounter, no matter how intimate or casual, can have an effect on the incarnational system of another.

When we are violent and abusive with another, we make it particularly hard for that person's incarnational system to integrate properly. It is more likely he or she will incorporate the energies of violence, pain, fear, and trauma into the structure of the incarnational system, which in turn draws on the least whole parts of each "team member." The World Self becomes more survival oriented and predatory, the "Human Self" aligns with that part of the collective human energy field that stores and then re-expresses pain and trauma, the personality becomes more separate, divisive, fearful, selfish, and defensive, and the soul becomes more withdrawn, unable to connect with or break through the negative vibrations. Such a person then becomes a source of violence himself or herself, continuing the affliction and passing it on to others.

On the other hand, when we can stand in our own integrated and holistic presence and know our own Self-Light and the sacredness that is within us, and we can relate to others with love, compassion, honoring, respect, kindness, and equanimity, then we can create a condition that makes it easier for them to find their own internal integration and wholeness.

In short, as co-incarnates, we can bring Light or evil into the world depending on how we relate to others. We can make it easier or harder for others to find integration, coherence and wholeness in their own incarnational system. We can help turn them into teams for goodness or teams for abuse, and others can do the same to us.

Of course there's nothing inevitable about this. A close friend of mine went through years of childhood abuse and ended up a wise, loving and very balanced individual helping others find healing in their lives. If any of the parts of Team Self are strong enough in their ability to forge an integrated whole within the incarnational system and give expression to an "I" that is both aligned with the earth and aligned with the heavens, aligned with self and aligned with spirit and sacredness, then the negative effects of others can be thrown off.

The I that Emerges

One way to look at Team Self and our INCarnation is to say that when we come to this world, we do so in partnership with larger collective presences. Our incarnations help to incarnate Gaia and also help to incarnate Humanity. We each take on some bit of the world and some bit of humanity and help to give it form. This is the Gaia within us and the Humanity within us, the "World Self" and the "Human Self." At the same time we are also incarnating the overall purpose and beingness of our souls and the specific set of potentials and possibilities that make up our unique individual lives.

It's the interaction of these four "partners" that creates the field that allows the incarnate world to receive and hold the fiery plasma of our sacredness. These four jointly create the "magnetic bottle" of our incarnation.

But which of these is really us? Where or who am I in the midst of this team?

From my perspective, we're none of the above and all of the above. We are the self, the I, that emerges from this system, or put another way, we are the whole system, which is greater than the sum of its parts. Ideally, we are not wholly a personality, not wholly a soul, not wholly caught up in the instinctual energies of the earth nor the collective energies of humanity; what we are is the whole that embraces, connects and engages all of them.

I want to repeat here that these four elements—soul, personality, world, and humanity—are in a way simply tokens; the incarnational system could be described using different sets of contributing elements. The main point is that there is a system and something emerges from it that was not there before. It's this something that is our personhood and our presence.

If we take a moment to reflect, we can feel these elements within us. We can feel the soul, for instance; we can feel our personal nature; we can feel the human elements and the natural forces and instincts. We would not exist if any one of them were removed. At the same time, we are not any one of them; we are all of them combined, an emergent presence and consciousness.

In Incarnational Spirituality, the emphasis is not on self-development that focuses on the personality nor is it on spiritual development that focuses on the soul. Both of these can be important, but they can also create a lack of integration and coherency within the whole system if they are pursued exclusively. In Incarnational Spirituality, the emphasis is on our presence, our emergent self.

This emergent self is not necessarily perfect or whole. As I said in the previous section, if the incarnational system is unable to achieve integration and wholeness, either because of internal disharmonies or the negative and hurtful influences of others, the emergent self will reflect this brokenness. What emerges is a self that embodies and expresses pain and woundedness rather than integration and wholeness. Unfortunately we live in human societies that are more prone to cultivating this broken kind of emergence than nurturing one that is truly integrated and whole, often through ignorance more than actual abuse and violence.

For example, there is a tendency in religious and spiritual thought to go "transpersonal," to give privilege and power to realms and beings of consciousness and life in the "vertical" or higher realms of being. Psychology, on the other hand, has a tendency to go "subpersonal," with an emphasis on the unconscious and subconscious dynamics within the human being.

In either case, the conscious, everyday personal self ends up on the short end of the stick, speaking generally. It either isn't as good or true or real as the transpersonal or it's less powerful than and is controlled and run by the subpersonal. It's as if the personal emergent self has been tag-teamed by two powerful entities, the transpersonal superconsciousness on the one hand and the unconscious subconsciousness on the other. One result has been to disempower us on a personal, conscious, everyday level. This can definitely have an effect on the ease with which a person can find integration within his or her incarnational system and express wholeness as an emergent self.

To make matters worse, these internal relationships are often couched in terms of conflict and opposition, with the personality being seen as the adversary of the higher spiritual self, dragging it down into the "mud" of the earth, or as the adversary of the subconscious as it struggles for dominance against powerful instinctive, unconscious urges. Paradoxically, such an adversarial approach can create the very opposition it imagines. It can make it more difficult for Team Self to coalesce and cohere in wholeness; it can create an opening for the most limited aspects of the human collective field and our biological natures to take over and act without proper integration and balance. The assumption of conflict creates the reality of a self that becomes an agent of conflict with the world as well as within itself.

The role of Incarnational Spirituality is to defuse this conflict and instill a sense of partnership. It is to honor and value the nature and role of the conscious, personal self as a mediator in collaboration with the superconsciousness (the soul) and the subconsciousness (the "Human Self" and the "World Self"). It seeks to restore the sense of dignity and power to the personal emergent self.

Rather than emphasizing the conflict between these different levels and elements, Incarnational Spirituality sees them as a partnership-in-the-making and views the personal self as a point of power that can make the decisions that make this partnership work. We can decide holopoietically for integration and coherency and set up the inner conditions for the other partners in our Team Self (or, if you prefer psychological language, for the superconscious and the subconscious) to blend and work together to create harmony.

We already have many tools and processes well established within religion and spirituality on the one hand to work specifically with the soul and other higher levels of consciousness and psychology on the other hand to work with the subconscious and collective levels of consciousness. Incarnational Spirituality doesn't have to recreate these tools or processes, though it does have tools of its own. What it does is to establish a new context in which to use these tools and a new purpose for their use: not to bring one part of our "system" into dominance over the others but to create a truly co-creative, collaborative, integrated, coherent partnership within us. The emergent self is this partnership in action.

In particular, it's this emergent presence that has the ability to foster and maintain integration and coherency. It can make the holopoietic choices, the decisions that produce wholeness. Is the personality too selfish? We can choose to balance it by attuning to the universality of the soul. Are we becoming too transpersonal, losing touch with the earth? We can balance this by paying more attention to our personal life and affairs. Are we too caught up in the human word? We can seek balance by engaging with nature. Are we losing touch with our humanity through our over-attachment to the non-human domains of nature? We can choose to restore and nurture our human contacts.

In all these cases, it is our emergent personal self that can make these choices. This is the presence that arises from the system and knows how to hold it and nurture it, creating wholeness. This is the presence that can attune to and embody the incarnational intelligence. It is this presence that is the fruit of our incarnation, and it's what Incarnational Spirituality seeks to nurture.

Going back to the image of a broken system as a source of evil, when the emergent self comes out of and expresses such brokenness, it loses the power to draw the best out of its team or to foster partnership. It draws too heavily on one or another of the team members, metaphorically speaking, and in so doing it ends up embodying imbalance rather than wholeness. In fact, its place as the integrative presence may be usurped by one or another of the parts. What then "emerges" isn't a true blend of all the elements within the incarnational system but one element in particular now becoming dominant.

The "team member" that can most help correct this situation and enable a balanced and coherent "I" to emerge is the soul. Attunement to the soul is a critical part of an incarnational practice. But what is the soul?

The Soul

The soul is like the boy or girl who brings a ball to a playground and organizes a game of soccer. The ball enables the game to take place: no soccer ball, no soccer game. But once the game has started, the owner of the ball simply becomes one of the players and part of a team. This is probably not how the soul is visualized by many people, but it is consistent with my experience. It has been my observation over many years that this partnership arrangement—the manifestation of "Team Self" —generates creative energy in ways that a more linear, hierarchical, authoritarian, top-down arrangement cannot do. A sun-satellite system in which there is a central authority that dictates and directs and everyone else simply reflects and obeys has structure and order and can be very clean and clear in its operation; there is certainly a place for such an arrangement in the scheme of things. But it's not always as creative or generative as an alliance of individuals who, though not necessarily equal in skill or abilities, all contribute insights and information to the emerging whole.

If any part of the incarnational system bears responsibility for what occurs in our lives, it is our personal, incarnate, everyday identity. We are the ones who experience the consequences of our choices and actions here on earth, and thus we are the "local" operational authority.

However, what the soul brings to the mix is uniquely important as it is the source of the qualities and energies that make Team Self possible in the first place, just like the child with the ball makes the soccer game possible. In particular, what the soul brings is the quality of coherence that holds the incarnational system together; the name we often give to this quality is love.

Though it may seem counterintuitive to say so—and it goes against much popular imagery about the "density" of the physical realm—the incarnate domain is very fluid. In some ways, it is more fluid or at least more volatile in its nature, than the subtle realms that surround it. This isn't because the structure and substance of matter itself is more fluid; it truly is denser than the subtle realms. What creates the fluidity is the presence of so much difference and thus of so many vectors.

Here's a metaphor for what I mean. Imagine a group of people who share the same origins, the same beliefs, the same outlook on life, the same likes and dislikes. It is easier to predict what this group is going to do and how it will behave. It has a stability based on its coherency. If you put a group like this in a room and show them pictures of a number of things and measure their responses, you are likely to come up with a statistical unity, that is, any given picture will elicit the same response in most if not all of the group members. There is a solidity of opinion and insight here.

But now take a group of individuals who are very different from each other. Each has a different origin, belongs to a different culture, has a different background, and different likes and dislikes.

Each person is very much a unique individual. Now you cannot predict as easily how this group will act or respond to specific stimuli. Show this group the same series of pictures and you are likely to get a wide spectrum of responses. The influence of all the different intentions and desires, thoughts and feelings in this group creates a volatile and fluid situation.

In researching the process of incarnation, I was told more than once that incarnation was like building a house made of toothpicks on the surface of a flowing river. It is a process in which the initiating intent does not necessarily work out exactly as planned. Skill is involved, and one must have knowledge of how the river flows and how toothpicks fit together, but there can still be unexpected change. The soul is not all-powerful, and mistakes can be made.

If I were to put the metaphor of Team Self into this context, then the process of building a toothpick house on a river is assisted by a River Intelligence that understands the river and its qualities of wetness and flow, a Toothpick Intelligence that understands the nature and structure of toothpicks, and a House Intelligence that emerges as the assembling takes place and that understands the nature of houses. In this process, the gift which the soul brings is to provide the holding that enables the river, the toothpicks and the house to work together without the whole thing collapsing or being swept away.

Given all the "moving parts" that go into an incarnation—all the diverse elements on many levels that must come together and work together—it's not surprising that some incarnations may not turn out perfectly. What is amazing is how well the system works overall. That there is violence and suffering in the world shows just how hard it can be to arrange toothpicks on rivers. That there is love and beauty, grace and joy, generosity and compassion, community and creativity shows how skilled our souls really are at managing it. Not yet perfect, but we're making progress!

Let me change the metaphor here. Imagine that you're spending a sunny day at the beach. You decide to build a sand castle. The problem is that all the grains of sand don't adhere very well, so they constantly slip and slide, causing your construction to fall apart. What do you do? Well, you get a bucket and bring up some sea water and moisten the sand. When sand is wet, it coheres. It sticks together, and sticky sand is just what you need to make your sand castle.

What the soul brings into the incarnate realm—the realm of boundaries and particles, difference and individuation—is love. Love is the active quality of holding and coherence. It connects and it integrates. It is holopoietic.

Love is at the heart of every incarnation. Love simply makes incarnation possible.

Further, each incarnation is potentially like a bucket, holding the sea water—the love—that can help other people build their sand castles, too. In other words, one of the purposes of incarnation is to be a holopoietic, integrative, coherency-creating, wholeness-producing force in the world. We carry water for our own sand castle—our own self and incarnational system—and we carry water to help everyone else (and everything else) in finding wholeness in and around their own incarnations. In effect, we serve the incarnation and wholeness—the sand castle building—of the world as a whole. And we draw on the water that others bring.

This is the power of the soul. It is that which holds and brings love into the world, and incarnation is its bucket.

Sovereignty

Sovereignty is a key concept in Incarnational Spirituality. A vital incarnational practice is to "stand in your sovereignty." But just what does this mean?

In my online dictionary, sovereignty is defined as "possessing supreme and independent power and authority in government." I define it simply as the capacity to be self-governing and the ability to make choices for oneself.

But it's more than just that. Sovereignty is the name I give to the integrative power that draws the incarnational system together and links it to the holopoietic presence and wisdom of the soul. It is, in a manner of speaking, the organizational principle that determines coherence and allows Team Self to manifest. It is the binding that holds the bucket together.

Going back to the metaphor of the soccer game, sovereignty is the ball itself. The whole game revolves around the ball: kicking it, making goals with it, preventing it from getting into the goal, and so on. Soccer is a game of football. Incarnation is a game of sovereignty.

Sovereignty is the active expression of the incarnational impulse within us, particularly as it translates the spacious, multi-dimensional, highly energetic nature of the soul into the three-dimensional, particular, individuated nature of the incarnate self. To violate another's sovereignty—or one's own, for that matter—is to risk making this impulse incoherent, causing the incarnational system to lose its integrity and risk a systemic breakdown into imbalance.

Again, we can illustrate this with our soccer game. There is no game without the soccer ball, but there's also no game if one person hogs the ball and doesn't let others play with it, too. A good game emerges when everyone has access to the ball and each person can kick it or run with it in his or her own way. The game ends if one person claims exclusive right to kick or handle the ball and no one else can do so.

We experience sovereignty as a personal state, but in fact it's a universal impulse. By this I mean that I cannot damage or disrupt your sovereignty without doing the same to mine. My sovereignty is not an excuse to attempt to dominate you; rather, I enhance my sovereignty, my coherency, my wholeness, by enhancing yours.

In December of 1963, the Rev. Dr. Martin Luther King, Jr. gave a talk at Western Michigan University. Its topic was "social justice and the emerging new age." In it he said:

> "All I'm saying is simply this, that all life is interrelated, that somehow we're caught in an inescapable network of mutuality tied in a single garment of destiny. Whatever affects one directly affects all indirectly. For some strange reason, I can never be what I ought to be until you are what you ought to be. You can never be what you ought to be until I am what I ought to be. This is the interrelated structure of reality."

This is a perfect expression of the nature of sovereignty as well. I am not fully free to be self-governing unless you are equally free in the same way. All sovereignty, like all life, is interrelated and interdependent. Perhaps we can see this if we return to the metaphor of the building a toothpick house on a flowing river. Sovereignty is the state of balance that holds the toothpicks together in the shape of a house. Imagine how much easier it is to maintain this if we are all helping each other in holding the toothpicks; we might as well, since we are certainly all in the same river!

Self-Light

Self-Light is the radiance of spiritual energy that arises from the act of creating Team Self. The soul is a high-energy phenomenon. It exists at a higher rate of vibration and a higher concentration of subtle energy and consciousness than we normally experience here in the incarnate realms. This is like saying that the soul stands on the top of a high hill, and the incarnate realm is at the bottom of that hill.

Imagine two people, one standing at the top and the other at the bottom of a hill. The one at the top represents a great deal of potential energy relative to the one at the bottom. Now the person at the top runs down the hill and leaps into the arms of the one at the bottom. During that run, all that potential energy is translated into kinetic energy. If you've ever experienced this, you know that the one at the bottom is going to be hit with a great deal of force due to the momentum of the one running down the hill.

When the soul gives its presence and energy to the process of creating an incarnational system, it's just as if it had run down a hill. The spiritual equivalent of kinetic energy is produced. Where does this energy go? It is released as a unique radiance of spiritual presence around the individual. This is that person's "Self-Light."

As my Lorian colleague Freya Secrest says, Self-Light is not simply a kind of "mini-transpersonal Light." It is a distinct form of Light in itself, an incarnational Light given unique characteristics and accessibility by the personal dimension. This is important to understand. We think of Light as something unitary, as if it were the same phenomenon wherever and whenever it is encountered. But in fact, Light—the fundamental spiritual energy of creation—comes in different flavors and frequencies. In this sense, it is similar to the different colors that can emerge through a prism from white light, or even more clearly, to the different frequencies of radiant energy that make up the electromagnetic spectrum. The electromagnetic spectrum is a single phenomenon but it also manifests as a range of specific, individual frequencies from very long radio and microwaves at one end to very short x-rays and gamma rays at the other.

As an incarnate person, there is Light that comes to me from many sources: from the Sacred itself, from my own soul and other transpersonal sources, from other people, and from the world around me. But there is also Light that I generate, Light that originates from me as a source. It does so not as the effect of any particular spiritual practice or development but as a product of the incarnational process itself. In my book, Blessing: The Art and the Practice, I call it our "empersonal spirit". It is quite simply the Light that emerges from the act of being a personal Self.

Besides possessing the same qualities as any other kind of spiritual energy or Light can offer, Self-Light particularly offers two things. First, it is a form of spiritual energy that is already configured to the incarnate realm and to the physical plane, so much so in fact that we may overlook it because it can feel familiar to us. Light from transcendent realms can be "rich" and powerful and hard to hold and digest without training; it comes to us from a higher energy source. It's like the person running down the hill and leaping into our arms to hug us; we may be bowled over. But Self-Light is like a person standing next to us turning and giving us a hug. Their energy is equivalent to our own; we are not knocked over.

Getting knocked over can be dramatic; it's something we can't help but notice. Getting a quick hug seems more ordinary and not so dramatic; we may forget about it. But both kinds of hugs offer us something. It's just that the ordinary hug is easier to assimilate while standing on our feet!

Self-Light is sacredness pre-digested by the incarnational process; it is the Soul's Light, a transcendent Light, digested and made available, like honey, by the incarnational process and the incarnational system. It is a form of spiritual energy that we can offer to each other freely and easily just as we are, and one that we can receive without a lot of fuss and bother. It is like a soft illumination rather than the stark glare of a lightning bolt. It's not very dramatic, but it can be very healing, nurturing, and empowering.

The second thing that the Self-Light experience offers is the realization that we are sources. We so often think of ourselves as recipients of Light from outside us that it can be a real shift of perception and self-understanding—an empowering shift at that—to know that we are also generators of Light. We are not just consumers. We are producers, too. We are not just planets reflecting the light from somewhere else. We are stars giving light out to the universe.

The Generative Star of Self

There is a question that is often asked in beginning astronomy or science classes: where is the nearest star? Many people try to remember which of the many star systems is closest to us (it's Alpha Centauri, which is about four and a half light years away), but this is a trick question. The correct answer is our own sun, which, of course, is also a star and is only eight light minutes away.

In incarnational spirituality, there is yet another answer to this question. The nearest star to you is actually...yourself.

A star is a perfect symbol of a generative source. It doesn't reflect, it produces. It gives off light and warmth. There are bright stars and dim stars, giant stars and dwarf stars, but they all are generative, fueled by the same nuclear processes within their core. The heart of a star is like a womb for the cosmos. In the extreme heat and pressure, heavier and more complex atoms are forged. These heavy atoms—such as oxygen, carbon, iron, and sodium—are the building blocks for planets and for life as we know it. Without the fusion taking place in the heart of stars that allows these substances to come into being, our universe would not exist.

In an analogous way, each of us is like a star, fueled from within by the self-creating and holopoietic processes of incarnation itself and generating an indigenous radiance, our own individual Self-Light. And as we take the raw emotional and mental energies of the world and "fuse" them within our own minds and hearts through our compassion, wonderment, curiosity, enthusiasm, and mindfulness, we can generate the more complex "atoms" of love, wisdom, insights, and creativity which can inspire others to be creative as well.

Like stars, we are each generators of the energetic substances from which our world can be built and shaped. When we fully understand this, we shift in our attitudes and thinking from being primarily consumers and receivers to being contributors and sources. This is an important and necessary shift in the practice of incarnational spirituality. It not only empowers us, but it adds a new dimension to our personal identities.

Self and the Incarnational Vision

At a time when our future is shadowed by physical challenges of global proportion, it's important that we are able to bring the full resources of our spirits, our minds, our hearts, and our bodies, as well as our best collaborative collective efforts, to bear upon the problems and opportunities that face us. We can positively shape our future but only if we are present to each other and to the earth in holistic ways.

In this historical moment, we are not served by philosophies that belittle or demean the incarnational state. We are not helped by teachings that create conflicts within us or that turn us away from the earth in search of a paradisiacal state elsewhere. We are not empowered by attitudes that place a limit on what a human being is or is capable of becoming. We are diminished by habits and actions that do not give scope for the full range of generative, creative, and loving expressions of which we are capable.

In short, we are undermined and our future is made less sure by anything that makes us less capable of incarnating in fullness and joy upon this world.

Whatever the ultimate nature of the self, it is the focal point of consciousness with which and through which we engage with the world. We do not meet the world as an abstraction; each of us engages with it as "me," as a distinct presence who brings difference and particularity into the world as creative tools for emergence. Whoever or whatever we are beyond this earth, we are here as agents of incarnational integrity and coherency, producers of wholeness, and sources of subtle energies from which the world weaves itself and its destiny.

This is the incarnational vision.

EXERCISES FOR CHAPTER TWO

PRESENCE EXERCISE

This is one of the earliest of the exercises I developed for Incarnational Spirituality. Its purpose is to create a felt sense of that part of you that draws all the elements of your incarnational system into a wholeness. Presence is the expression of that state of wholeness, incorporating both personal and transpersonal elements.

Important note: In part of this exercise, you are asked to attune to your everyday personal self. This is not an exercise in judgment or self-criticism. There may be things you don't like about yourself, are ashamed of, and wish to change or improve. That is perfectly fine, but that perception is not part of this particular exercise. You may certainly make an honest appraisal of yourself; indeed, this is essential. But do not get into self-blame or criticism or begin listing ways in which you can change and do better. That is another kind of work you can engage in that at another time.

1. Find yourself a comfortable place to stand. This is a moving exercise, one in which you will be turning to face the four directions.

2. Imagine yourself in a sacred or magical circle, a protected and honored space—an emergence space--that is dedicated to this exercise.

3. Begin by doing the Standing exercise, affirming and grounding yourself in your Sovereignty and your Sacredness. When you feel ready, begin this Presence exercise which you will do while standing. Try to feel the flow of energy and love moving out from your holding into your standing and then into the actions of the Presence Exercise.

4. Choose any direction and face it. In this direction is a vision of your Everyday, Personal Self, your Personality. Take a moment

to reflect on your uniqueness as a person. Reflect on what defines you, what makes you different from others. This is your ordinary, everyday self. What does this mean to you? What energy does it carry for you? What do you feel in its presence? What is your felt sense of your personal self? Be honest in your appraisal, but do not engage in self-criticism.

With your hands over your heart, open your arms outward in a gesture of welcoming your Personality. Then draw your hands back to your heart, drawing the felt sense of your Everyday Self into the circle of your acceptance and your love, integrating it into the wholeness of your inner Team.

Take a moment to honor your personal, everyday self. Appreciate it, give it thanks for its contribution to the wholeness of who you are. It is one of the portals through which you connect to the world. Embrace it with your love.

5. Turn ninety degrees and face a second direction. In this direction is a vision of your Humanness, the part of you that connects you to the human species and to all human culture, creativity, and civilization. Take a moment to reflect on being human. Your humanity gives you various attributes and potentials not shared by other creatures on this earth. Your humanness makes you part of a planetary community of other human beings, part of the spiritual idea or archetype of Humanity. What does this mean to you? What energy does it carry for you? What do you feel in its presence? What is your felt sense of your humanness? Be honest in your appraisal, but do not engage in self-criticism. Humanity may have its faults and it may behave badly in the world, but that is not the focus here.

With your hands over your heart, open your arms outward in a gesture of welcoming your Humanity. Then draw your hands back to your heart, drawing the felt sense of your humanness into the circle of your acceptance and your love, integrating it into the wholeness of your inner Team.

Take a moment to honor your human self. Appreciate it, give it thanks for its contribution to the wholeness of who you are. Being human is another portal of connection you have with this world, another channel through which Sacredness—your sacredness—can flow and act. Embrace it with your love.

6. Turn ninety degrees and face a third direction. In this direction is a vision of your World Self, your Earthiness, the part of you that is connected to the physical world and to nature as a whole. Take a moment to reflect on being part of this world, part of the biosphere, part of the realm of physical matter, part of the Earth. This part of you connects you to the World Soul. It connects you to ecology, to nature, to plants and animals everywhere. It connects you to the land, to seas and mountains, plains and valleys, swamps and deserts. What does this mean to you? What energy does it carry for you? What do you feel in its presence? What is your felt sense of your earth nature?

With your hands over your heart, open your arms outward in a gesture of welcoming your World Self, your Earth Self. Then draw your hands back to your heart, drawing the felt sense of your biological nature and participation in the natural world into the circle of your acceptance and your love, integrating it into the wholeness of your inner Team.

Take a moment to honor your World self. Appreciate it, give it thanks for its contribution to the wholeness of who you are. It is another portal of connection you have with this world, another channel through which Sacredness—your sacredness—can flow and act. Embrace it with your love.

7. Turn ninety degrees and face a fourth direction. In this direction is a vision of your Soul, your Transpersonal Self, the part of you that is connected to the inner worlds and to transcendent states of communion and unity, spirit and creativity. Take a moment to reflect on being part of Spirit, part of a vast ecology of life and consciousness not limited to physical reality. What does this mean to you? What energy does it carry for you? What do you feel in its presence? What is your felt sense of your transpersonal nature? Be honest in your appraisal.

With your hands over your heart, open your arms outward

in a gesture of welcoming your Soul. Then draw your hands back to your heart, drawing the felt sense of your Soul into the circle of your acceptance and your love, integrating it into the wholeness of your inner Team.

Take a moment to honor your Soul, your Transpersonal Self. Appreciate it, give it thanks for its contribution to the wholeness of who you are. It is another portal of connection you have with this world, another channel through which Sacredness—your sacredness—can flow and act. Embrace it with your love.

8. Turn ninety degrees back to the direction you were facing when you started. At this time, turn your attention to yourself at the center of these four "Selves," these four elements and directions of your Incarnation: your personal self, your human self, your world self, your transpersonal self. You are the point of synthesis where they all meet, come together, blend, partner, cooperate, merge, and co-create wholeness. You are the Presence that connects, the Presence that creates wholeness.

Feel the energies of these four selves, these four directions, flowing into and through you, blending, merging, and creating an open, evocative, creative space within you. Feel what emerges from this space. Feel the holistic Presence of your unique incarnation and sovereignty rising around you and within you, enfolding you, supporting you, becoming you. Feel the Presence that embraces yet is larger than the four selves you have acknowledged and honored.

9. Stay in the circle feeling the reality and energy of your Presence for as long as feels comfortable to you. When you begin to feel restless, tired, or distracted, just give thanks. Give thanks to your wholeness, to your Presence, and to the Sacredness from which it emerges and which it represents within the ecology of your incarnate life. Absorb, integrate, and ground as much of the felt sense and energy of this Presence as you wish into your body, into your mind and feelings, into yourself, releasing any overflow into your surroundings. Then step forward out of your circle and into your day, thus ending this exercise.

SELF-LIGHT EXERCISES

Expanded Self-Light Exercise

There is a spiritual presence and radiance that is generated by the act of being a unique self, an individuation of sacredness. It is a Light that is born from the love and will behind your intent to manifest as an individual upon the earth, an intent that whatever its other specific characteristics may be reflects and expresses the primal will-to-be of the Generative Mystery. I call this your "Self-Light."

Discovering and coming to know your Self-Light—your own unique embodiment and radiance of spirit—is a life-long process, one that can bring great joy, wholeness, and peace. There are many ways this can be done. Here is one simple exercise:

Let your attention and consciousness move into what you experience as the center of your body. This might be your heart, it might be some other area. Feel yourself surrounded by the millions and millions of cells whose individual lives make up your life. Feel the power and wonder of those lives all blending and connecting to support your own. You are immersed in a community of life.

Feel the force and light of a presence that pervades this community, drawing it into unity, giving it one identity. This presence is you. It is the presence of your Self. It makes you one being, one identity. Its light fills all your cells and all the activities that unite them.

Let your attention and consciousness move more deeply into this presence, moving into a sphere of Light that radiates the energy which forms into your physical body. Just rest in this Light of your unique body and the Self that forms it. What does it feel like?

When you are ready, let your attention move more deeply into this Light, as if you are moving towards the source of this Self-Light. As you do so, you become aware of a deeper presence that holds and empowers your Self-Light. This is the Light of the Sacred, a Light that fosters all incarnation. You are an emergent form of this greater incarnational Light. Expressed through your individuality, this universal Light becomes your Self-Light.

When you are ready, let your awareness and attention move back from this deep Light into the radiance of your Self-Light. Feel the wonder and magic of being who you are, manifesting a unique identity and creative potential. Feel your connection to the Light that runs through all creation and the way you individuate it.

Let your Self-Light flow into your boundaries, supporting their integrity and power and nourishing the space they create that holds and protects your unique identity. Let your awareness return to your body. Feel your Self-Light permeating and uniting the presence of all your cells. Feel the wonder of your physical incarnation, of your mind and heart, your ability to think, feel, and to make choices. Feel the wonder of your spirit. Let yourself be surrounded by this Self-Light forming around you your personal aura of grace and blessing.

Standing in this Self-Light, go forth to meet your day.

Simple Self-Light Exercise

Begin by standing in your own Sovereignty via the Standing Exercise, standing in the felt sense of your unique identity and your connection to your soul and to the sacred. If you wish, you can imagine this Sovereignty as a "spine" of Light within you, an axis around which your physical and subtle bodies develop and align.

Imagine this spine of Light becoming brighter and brighter with the energy of your own incarnational process as it unfolds from the will of your Soul and the Life of the Sacred. As this Light becomes brighter within you, it expands from your Sovereignty and enfolds you.

Imagine yourself standing in an oval of Light emanating from your "spine" of Sovereignty and individuality, an oval that surrounds you on all sides, top and bottom, connecting you with the energies of the world. This is your Self-Light.

When Stars Meet

This is a third way of exploring and attuning to your Self-Light

Imagine a spiritual star at the center of the earth. It's a green star radiant with the power of planetary life. Imagine the light from this star rising up through the earth, surrounding you, bathing and nurturing the cells of your body and forming a chalice around you.

Imagine a spiritual star within the sun in the sky. It's a golden star radiant with the power of cosmic life. Imagine the light from this star descending from the heavens and pouring into the chalice of earthlight that surrounds you and fills your cells.

Where the green and golden lights of these two stars meet in you, a new star emerges, a radiant star of Self-Light, born of the blending of the individual and the universal, the planetary and the cosmic, the physical and the spiritual. This Self-Light surrounds you and fills you, radiating back down deep into the earth and out into space, connecting with the star below you and the star above you. You are a Chalice of Self-Light within a pillar of spiritual energy rising from the earth and descending from the cosmos.

Take a moment to feel this Self-Light within and around you, your connection to the earth, your connection to the cosmos, your connection to your own unique and radiant Self. Take a deep breath, drawing this Light into and throughout your body; breathe out, sending this Light out into your world. Filled with this Light of Self, attuned to heaven and earth, go about your day.

EXPLORING THE GENERATIVE SELF

This is not exactly an exercise, at least not like the ones that precede it. It's more an invitation to reflection. The idea behind it is that just as stars turn one kind of atom into another through nuclear fusion, thereby releasing heat and light, so we can transform mental and emotional subtle energies from one kind to another, thereby enhancing and releasing self-light.

The Inner Solar Womb

Throughout the day through contact with the world, through media, and through participating in collective fields of thought and feeling, we are exposed to a variety of subtle energies, some of them disturbed and negative. We might hear something on the news that makes us anxious or angry, or we may simply pick up on a wave of anxiety moving through the collective human fields and feel anxious ourselves. At such moments, we can take these disturbing, negative, or anxious energies and transform them. We can apply our will, our intention, to them, not resisting them but deliberately and mindfully holding and exposing these negative "atoms" of thought and feeling to positive thought and emotion. We can expose them to peace, to calm, to love, to forgiveness, to compassion. We can attune to our own inner Light, both our Self-Light and Light we invoke from transpersonal levels, and draw the negative energies into that attunement, letting the Light transform them.

When we do this, we begin to feel lighter. We can feel a difference, a shift of energies within us. Normally, we may think of this purely as a psychological phenomenon, but seen with subtle perception, there is an energy transformation occurring that is analogous to any energy transformation on the physical plane. Something new emerges and Light is released. We become a bit more radiant than we were before.

Try this out and experiment. If you watch the news and feel something disturbing, experiment with using your own inner "solar womb" to process and transform the subtle energies you feel and see what happens.

Your Inner "Chlorophyll"

This is a similar reflective exercise. Take a moment to think about, feel into, or in some manner comfortable to you attune to a positive, uplifting, spiritual source. It might be something beautiful you see, or something pleasing you hear; it might be a meditation, a prayer, an attunement to the sacred. It can be anything as long as you feel it exposes you to Light and to a radiant goodness. Soak this in just like a plant soaking in sunlight. Feel the energy this generates in you; feel the goodness that fills you.

Now turn that felt sense of Light and goodness into thoughts or feelings or even more specially, into actions. These should be specific: that is, thoughts about someone you know, feelings towards someone you know, and actions in your immediate environment. Basically, translate this good energy into thoughts, feelings, and actions of kindness and blessing. They don't need to be complex; just holding a door open for someone and doing so with a kind and generous heart can be a transforming act of kindness in that person's day.

We can look upon this process as psychological, and it certainly has a psychological component. But seen with subtle perception, when we do this, we soak up one kind of subtle energy and transform it into a state that can be "food" or nourishment for the well-being of another's energy. We can take the inspiration of the sacred and bind it into physical form through an act of kindness, much as a plant binds sunlight into physical sugars and carbohydrates through photosynthesis. We might call this process "theosynthesis."

Experiment with this and see what happens. In both these experiments, you are exploring how you, as a generative being, can transform and affect the subtle substances from which the earth is made.

Chapter Three: Earth's Subtle Ecology

Introduction

The earth as a totality includes both physical and non-physical domains. I call the latter the "subtle worlds." In their interactions they affect each other and the planet as a whole. How they do so is an area of study and practice for Incarnational Spirituality.

It may seem strange for an incarnational spirituality to deal with non-physical, non-incarnated dimensions of life. The reason it does so is that the earth is an incarnational system the same as we are. If I may speak of "Team Self," then it makes equal sense to acknowledge "Team Earth," a sentient system in which various elements collaborate to manifest the living planet.

I think of the non-physical realms as a second ecology of the world, a "subtle ecology." It is every bit as diverse and filled with life as the physical plane is; in fact, I would say even more so. If our material world has bioregions, I might think of the immaterial world as having "noösregions" or "psyche-regions," environments that are differentiated by states of consciousness and energy. I discuss these realms in more detail in my book, Subtle Worlds: An Explorer's Field Notes.

What I wish to do here is give an overview of how the subtle worlds fit into an incarnational context and the role they play in shaping our future.

A Second Ecology

There exists all around us, usually unseen and unheard, a second ecology. Every bit as diverse and filled with life as the ecology we see around us—the ecology of animals, plants and people, rivers and seas, mountains and valleys—this is a vast realm whose landscapes are shaped from consciousness and whose inhabitants wear bodies of energy, not matter.

This is the non-physical realm, a collection of worlds, dimensions, and levels of being whose existence has been known to humanity for millennia. It has been called by many names: the Inner Worlds, the Otherworld, the Higher Order Worlds, the Spiritual Realms, the Unseen Worlds, and the Vertical Worlds, to name a few. I usually refer to them as the Subtle Worlds. Among those who live in these non-physical realms are angels, devas, gods, goddesses, nature spirits, ancestors, inner plane teachers, and the spirits of the dead. And this is only scratching the surface!

For as long as there have been human beings, people have contacted, communed and engaged with their non-physical counterparts. They have sought help, guidance, protection, healing, spiritual teaching and uplift, inspiration, insights into the nature of reality, and sometimes simply companionship. Depending on the culture or the locality, such non-physical beings have been seen as benign and helpful, evil and mischievous, or neutral and mysterious—and sometimes as all three at once depending on their mood. The fact is their nature and their capabilities are not like ours on the physical plane, and this has generated both awe and fear and often misunderstanding as well. Like any ecology, there are places and beings within it that can be dangerous to the unwary, the foolish, and the unprepared, and there are places and beings that are nourishing, hospitable, and helpful.

The Dark Continent

One analogy to describe the subtle worlds might be that of the early days of the European exploration of Africa, the "Dark Continent." Depending on where they went these explorers found endless seas of sand, dense jungles, towering mountains, and extensive plains. Besides diverse environments, they also found diverse inhabitants: from the Stone Age Bushmen in the Kalahari Desert to the erudite scholars of the fabled university of ancient Timbuktu in the sub-Sahara, and from the 18-inch tall Pygmies of the jungle to the Maasai of the East African plains who are over six feet tall.

One could easily imagine one group of Europeans returning claiming that Africa was all desert because all they'd seen was the Sahara, while another said it was impenetrable rain forest and jungle, and one group saying Africans were all tiny people while another said they were giants. Yet, as exploration continued and investigators compared notes and experiences, all these various discoveries came together into the mosaic of one vast, interconnected continent.

Africa is tiny compared to the vast ecology that is the non-physical realms. It's no wonder that accounts of these realms and their inhabitants can vary or that means of exploration and contact vary as well, just as some explorers had to use camels to reach their African destinations while others used riverboats. We are dealing with living realms that are evolving as much as is the physical world. Yet for all the differences in what people may experience when contacting or exploring the subtle realms, even a cursory study of the literature about such contact reveals many overlapping and common patterns. The territory may be vast but it is not chaotic nor purely a matter of individualistic interpretation.

Imbalanced Views

In the past, our thinking about the inner worlds has often been marked by imbalance. On the one hand, we may put too much awe and emphasis on the power of the non-physical realms and the beings upon them, giving them too much importance relative to ourselves. We over-privilege them, seeing the inner worlds as the "real worlds" of which the physical earth is merely a reflection. With this attitude, we may devalue our human, physical experience and overvalue insights and thoughts that come from the non-physical realm, which we mistakenly view as being an unalloyed source of sublime insights and wisdom.

On the other hand, we are in a time and, if we live in the Western technological cultures, in a place that on the whole view the inner worlds as a non-existent fantasy and inner beings as fables right along with the Easter Bunny and the Tooth Fairy. Or when these realms and their denizens are accepted, it may be as entertaining phenomena or as psychological projections whose reality is entirely subjective though important as symbols emerging from the unconscious.

An Ecology

In my experience, the non-physical realms are neither all powerful and holy nor fantasies or psychological projections. What they are is a second ecology of the earth. This second ecology is unseen and unrecognized by most people today, but it's every bit as important to the wellbeing of the world as the physical ecology with which it is interconnected as fully as earthly bioregions are connected to each other.

I like the term "ecology" in this context as it suggests something natural and organic, living and evolving. That is precisely what the inner realms are. They are not supernatural states or heavenly realms detached from any organic reality. They are dimensions with characteristics we have chosen to identify as "spiritual" just as the material earth is a dimension whose characteristics we have chosen to call "physical."

This second ecology is part of the larger wholeness of the planet in which we move and live and have our being. We are always interacting with it even if we are not aware of this fact. It is the partner of the physical ecology we see around us all the time. Learning how to engage and collaborate with this second ecology through the formation of spiritual alliances is an important skill that can greatly enhance and bless our lives and the life of our world. It is a needed step in the creation of wholeness for all for whom the earth is home, whether in a body or out of it.

Mapping the Inner

There are many ways to map the inner worlds depending on where a person is coming from or how he or she is viewing this subtle ecology. And in important ways, it's also impossible to really map it for it's a fluid, dynamic and evolving environment. It's like trying to map the ocean. Oh, you can map the shorelines around the ocean and the contours of the ocean bed, but try mapping the ocean itself. You can certainly discern major currents, like the Gulf Stream, but even these move and shift depending on overall planetary conditions such as wind, water temperature and salinity. It's an environment of life and change.

Ocean as Metaphor

At the same time, there are large structural features that remain constant over long periods of time. If we were exploring the ocean itself, there would be recognizable zones, each of which has its own characteristics and require something different from us if we are to function within it. There is a similar phenomenon in the second ecology, and we can use the ocean as a metaphor to fashion a simple kind of map.

For example, there is the shoreline, the place where the ocean and the land meet. Here we may find lovely beaches and rocky shores, tidal pools and coral reefs. This is where life first emerged from the water to begin its adventures on land. It's a place of emergence, generativity, and interaction, and it has its equivalent within the second ecology, too, if we think of the land as everyday human awareness based on our physical consciousness.

Out from the shoreline and the beach are the coastal waters that cover the continental shelf, also known as the "shelf seas." This shelf area is itself divided into three geologically distinct areas, each with its own type of sea life. Then there comes the continental break, the edge of the continent where the land drops off, sometimes dramatically, towards the abyssal plain of the sea bottom, the region of the deep ocean.

In my experience, the subtle worlds are similar. There are areas that are close to our physical world, and the beings who live in these areas often interact with the minerals, plants, animals, and people who make up this world. Here we find the angelic beings who minister to humanity, as well as the "elementals," "nature spirits" and Devas, the great angels of nature; here we find the beings that inhabit and express through what we think of as weather, beings whose "bodies" are in the energies of clouds and wind. These parts of the subtle worlds are like the shelf seas that "lay" over the "continental shelf" of everyday life. But the further out we go, the less interaction there is, though in one way or another the reality and nature of the physical plane remain a point of reference for all the beings in this region of the subtle worlds.

One particular part of this inner "continental shelf" of vital interest to us are the post-mortem worlds. These are vast and varied, representing the various environments and conditions that people enter after physical death. In some ways, these are transitional realms, a place where we learn to grow our "gills" again so we can function and live in the ocean once more. They are the places where we can integrate the experiences of our physical life just passed and learn the skills necessary to function in a whole new non-physical environment. Once we do so, we move out of being "post-mortem" and into a new life as spiritual beings fully able to function in the various realms of the second ecology.

Like the continental rise where the land drops off towards the abyssal plain of the deep ocean, there comes a point where we find ourselves in the "Deep Inner," places where life and energy truly become multidimensional and cosmic, and the beings who live there have little if nothing to do, except in the most general way, with our physical world, though they may have a great deal to do with the second ecology itself as a whole.

I think of these as the vast, spacious areas where one encounters planetary and cosmic beings, some so exotic that it is difficult to perceive or comprehend them. These are beings of whom I have only the slightest understanding or awareness, and then often only with the help of intermediaries who, like submariners, aid me in entering the depths.

In my own personal map, as I describe in my book Subtle Worlds, I divide this subtle ecology into three great zones. The closest to us—and thus the equivalent of the shoreline with its beaches and tidal pools in my ocean metaphor, is what I call the subtle environment. The farthest from us in vibration, energy and the very architecture of consciousness—and therefore corresponding to the deep ocean in our metaphor—are what I call the Higher Order Worlds. Here we find the higher angels and Devas and the highly evolved ancestors, teachers, guardians and guides of humanity.

Then in-between, corresponding to the "shelf seas," are a variety of realms and domains that collectively I call the Transitional Worlds, the home of many types of angels, Devas, nature spirits, and the like whose function is to mediate between the incarnate world and the Higher Order Worlds.

Mer-People, World People

In a way we are like the fabled mer-people and silkies of legend and folklore. These are creatures who live in the ocean but who can shed their tails and skins and put on human flesh and walk amongst us on the land. Our souls are denizens of the Higher Order Worlds, part of the "Deep Ocean" of my metaphor. Incarnation is a process by which we "come ashore," so to speak, and take on human form to walk the land of the physical realm and its associated states of consciousness. Yet always part of us is the hidden tail or magic skin that lets us return to the ocean and swim in its depths, and when we die, we set aside our human form and return to the larger ocean from which we originally came.

An important implication of this is that even though we are incarnated physically, part of us remains in touch with—and indeed part of—the subtle half of the world. Though most of us forget that we have ourselves a "second half" that exists in a non-physical dimension, it is there nonetheless. We are not in either one world or the other; we are always in both.

In this sense the "mer-people" metaphor is flawed for it suggests that we are only visitors on the land and that our true home is in the ocean. The fact is that the whole earth, seen and unseen, physical and non-physical, land and sea, is our home. We simply wear different skins depending on where we are living and acting in the moment, but we possess and can use many such skins. We are really not simply land people or ocean people; we are world people.

The Subtle Environment

The subtle environment is made up of all the subtle energy

fields you move around within during the day much like a fish moving through the ocean. This is where we find the auras and subtle energy fields that surround individuals, plants, animals and the various objects that make up our life. It is the area where we find the action of the subtle energies that have been named chi and prana, an area sometimes called the "etheric plane." It is also where we encounter the inner conditions created by human thought, feeling and imagination, often referred to in esoteric literature as the "astral plane." Your own subtle energy field, the product of your incarnational system, is constantly interacting with this environment, giving and receiving impulses and waves of mental, emotional, spiritual, and vital forces.

This subtle environment is the seashore where the tides and energies of the subtle worlds themselves meet the physical world and its mental and emotional counterparts. As such it is the beginning place for making contact and forming alliances with non-physical allies. It is also the primary field within which energy hygiene and subtle activism takes place, processes I'll discuss more fully in a later chapter.

The Local "Beach"

Each of us is surrounded by our own subtle energy field or aura which is permeated by our Self-Light. This field is shaped and affected by the quality and nature of our thoughts and feelings. This field is like an energetic "skin" and serves as the first point of contact with most subtle energies in our environments. The condition of our own field affects the nature and quality of this contact. If I am peaceful and calm, then there is no personal turbulence, so to speak, to roil or distort the subtle energy field around me; on the other hand, if I am in personal turmoil, depressed, angry, fearful, and so forth, these qualities may not only be projected into my immediate energy surroundings, but may shape that environment the way a wind can whip up waves on an otherwise clear lake. This is why in nearly all spiritual traditions and practices, emphasis is placed on learning to still the mind and calm the heart.

If I use the metaphor of the subtle environment being like the seashore where the ocean meets the land, the closest "beach" beyond the boundaries of your own energy field is the one made up of the subtle energies immediately around you. This environment in many ways mirrors the physical world and certainly interacts with it; these interactions can keep this subtle environment in flux, though how dynamic and changing it is depends on the overall circumstances and surroundings and the nature of those interactions.

Just like the ecology at the beach can be complex, this is equally true for the "subtle beach." There are five main types of phenomena that make up the ecology of the subtle environment. These are fields, waves, beings, thought forms, and "seeds."

Fields are subtle energy phenomena that form around people, creatures, plants, and things. Everything has an emanation of subtle energy that constitutes its "personal field."

Waves are currents of energy from the subtle worlds that ebb and flow just like tides that come from the physical ocean as well as currents that are set into motion by physical plane events or by the individual and collective impact of human thought and feeling upon the subtle environment.

Beings are living entities that either live in or work in the subtle environment; a fairly common example would be those beings who work directly with the vital energies of plants and which are often called "nature spirits." And just as whales can come from the deep ocean close to shore, so beings from the Higher Order Worlds and the Transitional Realms use the subtle environment as a place of contact with the incarnate world.

Thought-forms are constellations of energy molded around particular thoughts and images, usually but not always originating with human beings. Most of them are very short-lived, coming into existence as a person thinks strongly or emotively about something and then fading into non-existence as that person thinks or feels strongly about something else. But if consistent thought, imagination and energy are put into a particular thought form, it can develop an autonomous and long-lasting existence.

"Seeds" is my term for unfolding events that have not yet

63

manifested in the physical world but unless something changes or "uproots" them, they will do so. They are the potentialities of the future existing in an energy form en route to be realized in physical space. Sometimes these seeds are also thought forms, but mostly they are "vectors" of possibility and potential: configurations of energy moving in a particular direction with particular intent and "momentum." If we wish to use spiritual energies to influence the shape of the future, one way is by working with these seeds.

Of course, not all of these phenomena are everywhere present. But still the subtle environment is a rich, complex ecology the same as our physical environments can be. And the subtle environment is as much a place of incarnation for us as the material world around us; though invisible to most of us, it is an integral part of the world in which we live.

Subtle Worlds

If the subtle environment is like the seashore, then the subtle worlds are the ocean. If the ecology of the subtle environment is rich and complex, then this is even truer by many magnitudes for the subtle worlds themselves. I have already said that I divided these worlds into the Transitional Realms and the Higher Order Worlds, and if you'd like a more detailed discussion about them, then I recommend my book, Subtle Worlds: An Explorer's Field Guide.

The Wholeness of the World

In the previous chapter I wrote about Team Self and the need for integration and coherency. The same is true for the earth. We are all part of "Team World," and the holopoietic impulse to create wholeness and coherency is as strong and necessary on a planetary level as it is for individuals. Just as the subtle part of ourselves—our soul or transpersonal side—is an important part of the wholeness of Team Self, so the transpersonal or subtle side of the earth is important to our planetary wholeness.

When most people think of the subtle worlds, assuming they

accept that they exist, they think of them as sources for advice, guidance, blessing, help, and teaching. There is an emphasis on receiving messages of some kind. Such messages can be useful and inspiring, and there is no doubt that there are wisdom and insights, as well as love and blessings, to be had from the Higher Order Worlds and the Transitional Realms. But in my own experience, an important function of a relationship between a physical and non-physical being is to knit the two realms together and contribute to a greater degree of wholeness, coherency, and integration within the world. There is a need for an exchange of presence and energy even more than there is for an exchange of messages. There is a need for both sides to collaborate in partnership to experience and embody the wholeness of the earth and the integrity of Gaia.

In the context of Incarnational Spirituality, contact and work with the subtle worlds—whatever other purposes or needs it may serve—is ultimately about expressing a relationship that serves and enhances the wholeness of the world, as well as our own wholeness. On an operational level, this means doing such inner work in the context of a relationship with Gaia, the Soul of the World.

EXERCISES FOR CHAPTER THREE

Introduction

Learning to commune and interact with the subtle worlds is beyond the scope of this introductory book; it's certainly not a matter for an exercise or two. It's really a lifetime endeavor. There are many traditions that teach how to engage in this endeavor and "swim out" into the "ocean," to use the metaphor from the preceding Chapter and different techniques for different approaches and different kinds of people and cultural backgrounds.

In Incarnational Spirituality, we start with the sovereignty of the individual and the power of his or her unique generative nature, as we discussed in Chapter Two. Contact and communion with the subtle worlds need to enhance and not detract from our incarnational process. It is a collaborative process, not one of one party simply listening to and receiving guidance from another. Because of this, there is no single recipe in Incarnational Spirituality for all people to use for contacting the subtle worlds; there is no one or two exercises. It is a matter of mentoring and tailoring an approach that is right for you. This is what we seek to do in our classes

So the exercise that accompanies this chapter is not about contacting the subtle worlds. But it is about the place from which (or with which) such contact begins. It's about becoming mindful of one's own personal subtle energy field. Here is where our thoughts and feelings can become transformed into subtle energies which may then flow out into the larger world, and here's where the subtle energies of the world can become part of us, sometimes transforming into thoughts and feelings that we may think are our own. In some traditions, this field surrounding us is known as our "aura." Using the metaphor of the seashore, this is our own private beach where the sea meets the land. So I call this exercise "Going to the Beach."

GOING TO THE BEACH

1. Begin with the Standing Exercise, invoking the felt sense of

your own sovereignty.

2. Still standing, imagine an arms-length circle around you with you standing in the middle of it. You can extend your arms and hands and trace out this circle if you wish. Now imagine this circle expanding vertically, turning into a oval with you at the center. This oval around you represents your personal subtle energy field, your personal "beach" where your thoughts and feelings flow down from the highlands of your consciousness to meet the sea of subtle energies from the world. This oval is where you and the world meet energetically.

3. Imagine this oval as filled with a liquid, as if you are surrounded by a tank of water, for example. What is the state of this liquid as you attune to it? Is it moving, is it still, is it clear, is it dark, is it empty, is it full of things in suspension within it? Using your imagination and will, turn this liquid still and clear, like a calm lake. Surround yourself with stillness.

4. Imagine a source of Light above you. Imagine Light flowing down into your oval from the top, flowing through the clear liquid and exiting into the ground beneath your feet. Imagine a source of Light below you within the earth. Imagine a clear Light flowing up into your oval from beneath your feel, flowing through the clear liquid on the other side of the downward flow and exiting into the sky above your head. In this way you have a circulation between heaven and earth moving through and around the liquid in your oval. The oval connects you horizontally to the world and the circulation connects you vertically to the Higher Worlds and to the World Soul and the Light within the Earth.

5. In this exercise, you are not necessarily trying to think "good" thoughts and have "positive" feelings; rather, you are instilling a healthy flow and movement within your personal energy field, aligning and attuning it to the Light of the Higher Worlds and the Light within the Earth, and instilling a peaceful rhythm within your

67

field. Although a discipline of mindful thinking and feeling is also important, in this exercise the emphasis is on the quality of presence within this subtle field. In this way, whatever thoughts or feelings enter your field, either from within yourself or from the world around you, they don't become stuck in a stagnant or closed field but can become part of a circulation that can keep them transforming and moving towards an appropriate destination in an appropriate way.

You can at different times during the day also do the "When Stars Meet" exercise from the last Chapter, opening your own inner generative source of Self-Light and letting that Light fill your subtle energy field as well.

CLEANSING HANDS (Energy Hygiene)

This is a simple exercise of personal energy hygiene you can do anytime to help cleanse your personal energy field or aura. (For a fuller explanation of energy hygiene, please see Chapter 5.) Begin by directing a flow of love into your hands. See this love as arising from all parts of your body, not just from your heart center. In other words, imagine that every part of your body is making its own contribution to this loving energy.

As you do this, you most likely will feel some sensation in your hands. Your hands might grow warm, for example, or you may feel a tingle in them or a sense of something flowing along your fingers. And you may feel nothing at all, which doesn't mean that nothing is happening. It is the intention that is most important here.

When you feel ready, imagine your personal subtle energy field as an oval around you as in the preceding exercise. Then put your hands into this field and move them about. It's as if you're stirring a soup or setting the water in a pond in motion. Imagine your hands channeling love into all parts of your energy field as you move them about, up and down, back and forth, in front of you, to the sides, and in back of you. You're not trying to move the energy of your field in a particular direction, you are simply stirring it up with love.

At some point as you do this, visualize the circulating flow described in the exercise above, the flow of Light from the Higher Worlds "down" into your field and the flow of Light from the Earth "up" into your field, creating a circulating flow. This flow of Light gathers up all the stirred up "stuff" and moves it out, carrying it to an appropriate destination for healing or transformation.

Finally, end with a combination of the Standing and Where Stars Meet exercise, affirming your sovereignty and Self-Light and letting the warmth and love and light of your Self-Light pervade and bless your field. After you do this, imagine the "liquid" of your field, the energy within it, as once again calm, quiet, and clear, like a pure mountain stream and pool.

A Final Word

Your personal subtle energy field is the place where much (if not most) of the contact with subtle world beings, particularly within the subtle environment immediately around you, takes place. The principle mode of contact is to interact with your field. The quality of your field directly (and sometimes dramatically) affects the quality of the contact. If your field is turbulent, murky, filled with fearful thoughts and feelings, or with other negative qualities, then it's those qualities that may be reflected back to you. At the very least, a turbulent field can lead to misinterpretation of the material presented to you by an inner contact. Being able to create and hold a clear, calm field is not only very helpful in meeting the challenges of everyday life, it's essential to establishing good contact with the subtle worlds.

An introduction to

Chapter Four: Gaia

Gaia, The Soul of the World

Human beings are not the only ones with souls. If I think of a "soul" as a sentient field of life and energy existing within the Higher Order Worlds, then most things upon the earth, both organic and inorganic, either possess or are part of such a field. If this is true for some of the lowliest creatures and things on earth, it is also true for the most vast, which is the planet itself. The World Soul is the great life and consciousness that holds the entire living field of the earth, making possible both the coherency and shape of the planet and the existence of the biosphere that thrives upon it. I call this World Soul "Gaia." It is a presence that most assuredly can be perceived and contacted within the subtle worlds.

Gaia originally was the Greek name of the earth goddess. In recent years a British scientist named James Lovelock conceived the theory that the planet as a whole possessed the self-regulating dynamics of a living organism. In honor of the Greek goddess, he called this the "Gaia Theory." Since then the term "Gaia" has been taken up into the imagination and vocabulary of various environmental movements and groups and is now fairly common as a synonym for the world in its ecological wholeness.

There is some risk to calling this planetary being "Gaia." It can suggest a feminine "Mother Nature," and we may indeed be inclined to think of Gaia as a synonym for "Nature." But it is more than that. Gaia is as much the concrete and asphalt of the city as it is the meadows and forests of the countryside. It is brick and steel and mortar, and it is soil and water and air. If in any way it comes from the earth and is of the earth, then it is Gaia. It is the incarnating and holopoietic spirit of the world.

Gaia is not the Sacred. It is not the Generative Mystery from which all creation comes; it is neither a god nor a goddess, although to us it might seem like either. The power of Gaia is to enable life to exist on this world. Unlike Mars, the earth is not a barren world. It has a biosphere. The existence and growth of this biosphere with all its uncounted trillions of organisms from the tiniest microbe to the greatest whale is a manifestation of Gaia's presence and activity. Gaia radiates the energy of life. It is like a "green star."

The idea of Gaia can seem mystical or abstract. We may think that even if there is such a planetary being, its life is so vast and so different from our own as to put it outside the sphere of our everyday concerns. Perhaps the soul may have a relationship with such an entity, but what does that mean to our everyday lives?

One answer to this, and one of particular relevance to our future, is that if by Gaia we simply mean the integrity and health of the biosphere, then developing behaviors and a relationship with the world that supports that integrity and health is vitally important. If we disrupt or destroy the web of connections, interrelationships, and processes that make up the biosphere, then we will suffer consequences as our own well-being is part of the life of our world.

But Gaia is more than just another name for ecology or environmental integrity. If we think of it as a spirit of planetary wholeness—the identity that holds life on this world together just as my soul's identity, acting through the DNA of my cells, holds the life and integrity of my body together—then we come closer to understanding its relevance in our lives. The wholeness of Gaia is not something outside of us but within us as well. It is the spirit of our own wholeness, our own integration and coherency as organic, human beings who are natives of this world. To have a relationship with Gaia is to have a relationship with that which promotes and sustains wholeness in general and the wholeness of our human identities in particular.

Relationship

Incarnation is essentially about relationships. To put it in chemical terms, it's about forming strong molecular bonds that allow new elements and combinations to come into being. Some of these bonds or relationships need to be stable and long-lasting, like the bones in our body. They provide the scaffolding upon which and around which the incarnation develops. Other bonds or relationships are more fluid, even temporary, allowing for dynamic change and adaptation. We need both, the fixed and the fluid, to have the flexibility that life requires.

One of the key stable bonds or fixed relationships is that between the soul and its incarnate self. This incarnate self consists of the body, the subtle field, the personality and the emergent self that forms around and within these other three. This emergent self is the soul within the three-dimensional world, the incarnate world. As I have written, what I call sovereignty is the bond, the link, the relationship between these two aspects of soul, the incarnate and the transpersonal. One of the effects emerging from the dynamics of this relationship is a spiritual radiance—an emanation of energy—that I call our "Self-Light."

In any spiritual work, it's vital that this primary relationship or bond be acknowledged and strengthened. This is a key element of an incarnational spiritual practice.

A second vital bond or relationship is that which exists between the elements that make up the incarnational system or field, what I called "Team Self." In effect, this is really a collection of relationships between various elements that allows us to form the wholeness, coherence and integrity of our incarnate self. This brings our personal individual self into being as a womb within which an emergent self, an incarnate soul, can develop. Being able to love and honor one's self as an incarnate human individual is a key practice to strengthening this particular set of relationships.

The third key relationship is that between the individual soul and the World Soul or Gaia. This relationship is what opens the door to make incarnation possible in the first place and it's also one of the basic reasons for incarnation: we incarnate not only for our own benefit or for that of humanity but as part of the overall incarnation and development of Gaia itself.

The Gaian Relationship

The relationship with Gaia is a seminal one. From an incarnational standpoint, we would not—could not—be in this world without its assistance. Gaia forms the matrix of life from which the bodies we inhabit emerge. By the same token, our lives help to incarnate the potentials of life on this planet; we are part of Gaia's incarnation as well. We are co-incarnates. To relate to Gaia is to relate to the very processes that enable our incarnations to occur and to unfold. This essential bond is what I call the Gaian relationship. It enables the soul to form other more specific bonds with various elements of the world that then generate the specific ingredients of an incarnations; The Gaian relationship is part of the glue that brings an incarnational system into being. It is the link between the members of Team Self, as well as the link that allows us each to be a contributing part of Team Earth.

An Identity of Love

The Gaian relationship is a manifestation of the love and desire to serve that is exchanged between the individual soul and the World Soul. Because of this, each incarnation is an expression of that love. It is the way in which the love within the Gaian relationship is actualized. This is why, in my understanding, whatever other forces and reasons may lie behind a particular sojourn in the incarnate realms, the fundamental driving impulse is love.

This love is not an abstract, generalized, feel-good kind of emotion. It is a focused distillation of creative power, an expression of the will to good, the will to serve and to enable. We come to earth in the first place because its destiny, its life, its evolution, its wellbeing, its work is something we wish to support and be part of. And the earth welcomes us lovingly because it can contribute to and nourish the unfoldment, evolution, and wellbeing of our own kind of life and consciousness. It is a truly symbiotic relationship, and the soul is the concrete manifestation of this symbiosis.

We and Gaia are two very different kinds of life forms; we are at different levels of energy and consciousness, though it is not exactly accurate to say that Gaia is more evolved or "higher" than we are. The differences, and they are significant and important, are not necessarily measured in quite that way. We can do some things that Gaia cannot (just as a cell in my body can do some things that I cannot), and of course the reverse is true. Gaia obviously carries a pattern and field of energy and complexity far beyond what we do, and this needs to be taken into account. But this difference doesn't diminish us or the importance of what we can bring to Gaia as human souls and as incarnate human beings. It does not diminish the love that is at the heart of our relationship with this great planetary Being. I need my cells and my cells need me; Gaia needs its human partners and we need Gaia. We both benefit from the love we bring to each other.

The identity of love that is the soul is very potent. It makes the Gaian relationship possible and it is the generative "engine" that enables that relationship to do its work within the body of the world. We could say that the challenge of incarnation is to replicate or transfer this identity from the Higher Order Worlds where it originates into the three-dimensional, physical, mental and emotional realms where our incarnations take place. The emergent self or incarnational self has the challenge of rediscovering or remembering and then expressing this identity, this Gaian relationship, in the context of its everyday life.

One way we can do this is through the practice of creating what I call Grail Space.

Grail Space

The idea of Grail Space is really a simple one. Everything in our environment is generating a field just as we do. This is true whether we are talking about a plant, an animal, a person, or a thing such as a coffee cup, a sofa, or a desk. The nature, quality and dynamics of these fields will be different for sure, but the fields are there nonetheless. Grail Space, is a way of engaging with these local fields—with the objects, plants, animals, and people who are around us—in a manner that acknowledges the sacredness within them and enhances the shared capacity to hold and express such sacredness.

I use the term "Grail Space" to mean any space that holds sacredness, just as in legend the Holy Grail held the transformative blood of Christ. We live in Grail Space. The entire cosmos is the primal Grail Space holding the sacredness of the Generative Mystery. But this primal Grail Space can be accentuated in any specific local environment at any time through our deliberate and mindful actions.

The practice of creating a local Grail space is one of standing in our own presence and Self-Light and engaging the immediate environment around us to evoke more fully the Light that flows from the primal Grail Space, that is, from the Sacred itself. Fundamentally, this is a practice of extending love and acknowledgement to what is around us. It is an act of honoring and relating to our environment in such a way that it responds energetically to our presence, awakening and expressing its own Grail capacities. It is the act of mutual holding that turns the environment, with ourselves in it, into a Grail from which sacredness may shine forth.

The creation of Grail Space is a reciprocal act, not something we do to something else. It is an act of extending an invitation, allowing the environment to respond as fully as it can in the moment. Grail Space is born of relationship based on honoring the sovereignty and identity of all involved. It is not precisely the same as blessing what is around us, though it certainly can have that effect. What I mean, though, is that it's not a "sun-satellite" effect in which we provide the spiritual energies and presence and everything else simply soaks it up. Rather, Grail Space is based on the recognition that everything around us—every creature, plant, and object—is a "star" in its own right and has its own radiance of Light, presence and sacredness. It may be bright, it may be dim, it may be obvious, it may be hidden, but it's there. We live in a galaxy filled with infinite stars of Light right here on the earth.

You may initiate Grail Space by extending love and presence into your environment but you fully create it by acknowledging the light and sacredness that is already there in the things around you and inviting and welcoming that light and sacredness into your life as well. You receive as well as give, and you do so by seeing the world around you as a partner and potential ally, not as a needy sponge waiting to receive whatever spiritual benefits you may project.

Grail Space is also a way of engaging with the spirit of Gaia that manifests through all the elements of the world around us. In one sense, when we form Grail Space, we are forming it in partnership with Gaia. When we acknowledge and extend blessing to other creatures and things in our world, we are creating a presence of collaborative wholeness within the body of Gaia itself. This honors and nourishes the Gaian relationship as much as anything we do.

EXERCISES FOR CHAPTER FOUR

GRAIL SPACE

Creating Grail Space is really a simple process, but I break it down into a number of steps just so you can get a sense of the procedure. To read it, it can seem like a lot, but it's really a very fast, simple process. The main difference between this technique and simply sending love into your environment is the connection with the incarnational process and identity of everything about you in a partnership modality. You are joining with the Incarnational Light—the Light of Identity—within the things in your environment to create a mutually beneficial space or field into which sacredness may be invoked.

One way to think of this is as if everything in your environment is alive and a person and you are joining hands with them to form a great circle. This circle creates the Grail Space, and into it sacredness is invoked.

The Exercise

1. Begin by standing in your own Sovereignty, in the felt sense of your unique identity and your connection to your soul and to the sacred. If you wish, you can imagine this Sovereignty as a "spine" of Light within you, an axis around which your physical and subtle bodies develop and align.

2. Imagine this spine of Light becoming brighter and brighter with the energy of your own incarnational process as it unfolds from the love within your Soul and within the Sacred of which it is a part. As this Light becomes brighter within you, it expands and enfolds you.

3. Imagine yourself standing in an oval of Light emanating from your "spine" of Sovereignty and individuality, an oval that surrounds you on all sides, top and bottom, connecting you with the energies

of the world. It forms and radiates from you as a personal Grail, an incarnational field holding sacredness.

4. Take a moment to survey your immediate environment, taking note of all the things that are in it. Do so as a witness in a non-judgmental way, as if seeing these things for the first time with beginner's mind. You don't have to focus on each item separately but just take in the general arrangement, content and feel of the space around you.

5. Everything in your immediate environment is an expression of the Sacred. Everything you see participates in the primal Grail Space. Everything has within itself a "spine" of incarnational intent and Light, its own form of Sovereignty and identity. Imagine yourself surrounded with a multitude of "grails of Light" emanating from everything in the space around you. In your heart, acknowledge and give honor to the presence of all these "spines" or "grails" of incarnational and sacred Light.

6. Imagine your aura of Self-Light—your Grail of sacredness and incarnational Light—expanding into the room, joining in love with the myriad multitude of Lights all around you. Feel your Light augmenting and blending with the Lights around you, feel their Lights blending with an augmenting your own. You are forming a subtle partnership with your environment and everything seen and unseen within it. Feel this partnership turning your immediate, local environment into a Grail that you and all the things around you collaborate to create, a Grail you share.

7. The felt sense of this field and the partnership and "circle" of reciprocal energy that generates it is the Grail Space. It is a field of collaborative partnership and support in the incarnational process with everything around you in your local space, a partnership that can receive and hold a Presence of sacredness.

8. Standing in this Grail Space, acknowledge this Presence of

sacredness heightened in yourself and your environment. Imagine it being held in this space, and then overflowing into the larger world beyond, a source of energy, blessing, love, and life.

9. Stay in this Grail Space as long as feels comfortable. When you feel tired or restless, simply draw your Self-Light back into yourself, giving thanks to your energy partners for their participation. Imagine their incarnational light moving back into themselves as well, knowing the environment you share will resonate with the Light and Presence you have collectively invoked for as long as it is able. Stand in your Sovereignty, acknowledging your wholeness your integrity, your identity, and your connection to the Sacred. Then go about your daily affairs.

EARTH CORE, LIFE LIGHT

This exercise is another way of engaging with the felt sense of Gaia. It's based on the image that the Earth has two cores, a solid one of a nickel-iron alloy at the very center and a liquid, "outer core" of molten metal held at temperatures hotter than the surface of the sun. These rotate, and this rotation generates the magnetic field that surrounds the earth and protects us from harmful solar and cosmic radiation.

1. Imagine the solid core of the earth deep beneath your feet. Around it is a sphere of molten metal. As these turn, a magnetic field is generated, surrounding and embracing everything upon the earth. Take a moment to feel yourself held and embraced, protected and enfolded in this Earth field. You are not simply passive in this field. It impacts and energizes the natural fields of your own body, and as it does so, energy is generated and shaped within and around you as well. Feel the Earth empowering and energizing your body and your own energy field. Feel the energy radiating from you as a result of the relationship between your field and that of the planet.

2. Now imagine a star within the earth. This is the heart of the World Soul. As love pulses through it, it generates a field as well, a

field of love that embraces everything upon and within the planet. Feel yourself held and embraced, protected and enfolded in this loving field of the World Soul. You are not simply passive in this field. It impacts and energizes the natural fields of subtle energy around and within your own body. As it does so, a loving energy is generated and shaped within and around you as well. Feel this energy radiating from you as a result of the interaction and relationship between you and World Soul.

3. Finally, imagine the earth as a star. It's a green star, radiant and vibrant with life. It's the Star of Gaia, the biosphere. As life flows through it, it generates a field of life that embraces and holds everything upon and within the planet. Feel yourself held and embraced, protected and enfolded in this living field of Gaia. You are not simply passive in this field. It engages and interacts with the life and natural bioelectrical and biopsychic fields of your own body and as it does so, a living radiance is generated and shaped within and around you as well. Feel this subtle energy radiating from you as a result of the interaction and relationship between you and the living energy of Gaia and the biosphere.

Earth, Love, Life: These are the triple fields of energy that enfold and embrace you at all times, shaping and energizing the flow of your own energies. Attuning to them, feeling yourself held and bathed within them, can be a source of strength, wholeness, and energy hygiene. Your interaction with them generates energies within you, energies that become part of and nourish your Self-Light.

4. Go about your day alive and empowered by the knowledge that you are held and are interacting with these three great fields of activity and beingness in our world

An introduction to

Chapter Five: Working with the Subtle Half

Overview

Working with the non-physical or "subtle" dimensions of the world has numerous benefits when approached responsibly. At the simplest level, it helps us to reclaim the subtle aspects of our own lives, gaining the capacity to navigate the world in greater wholeness. It also holds the possibility enabling us to contribute in positive ways to conditions and areas of the world that need help or healing. This includes increasing our ability to affect and shape the future. The deepest reason, though, is that working with the subtle half of the world enhances the wholeness of all incarnations, including that of Gaia itself.

There are many ways a person might interact with the subtle half of the world and many reasons for doing so. In Incarnational Spirituality, we focus on three: energy hygiene, subtle activism, and collaborative mind. All of these are ways in which we can bless our environment and enhance our own activities.

All three of these are based on a "three-legged stool" that, from the perspective of Incarnational Spirituality, underlies all safe interactions with the world's subtle half or "subtle ecology." These three legs are sovereignty and individual presence, Grail Space, and attunement to Gaia. One could add a fourth leg, which is attunement to the Sacred, but in fact the other three are also manifestations of sacredness. The Standing Exercise and attunement to one's incarnational sovereignty is also an attunement to the sacredness within oneself. The creation of Grail Space with one's immediate environment is an attunement to the sacredness within that environment. And attunement to Gaia is attunement to the sacredness within the world. To attune to the Sacred as a separate presence, a "fourth leg of the stool," can be an important practice with its own unique benefits, and certainly adding it to the other three attunements is a matter of personal preference. But in so doing, it should not imply that the other three "legs" of the stool do not also embody and manifest the Sacred in their own particular ways. By "Sacred" here, I don't mean any particular religious image of God, though you can certainly use whatever image of deity is important to you and in which you believe. What I mean is a universal and inclusive source of life, wholeness and love, the Ground of All Being, which seeks to bless each individual life according to its uniqueness and its needs, enabling it to fulfill in optimal ways its potentials. This Presence can be sought out on its own but it is also an essential element within all existence, which is why I think of it as automatically part of the "three-legged stool."

I. ENERGY HYGIENE

We live in a world filled with energies of all kinds. Some are the electromagnetic forces that light our lights and heat our stoves and bring us voices over the radio and images on our televisions. But there are other energies that surround us as well, of which most of us are probably unaware but which can affect us just as powerfully. These are subtle forces generated by life, consciousness and spirit.

These forces are set into motion by things we do and feel and think, by our emotional and mental activity. There are subtle energies that radiate from our spiritual presence as well. At a physical level we experience these energies as the chi which martial artists use or the prana that is part of yoga.

These are meta-physical energies, and they are as much a part of our surroundings as the physical ones with which we are more familiar. They flow between people and between us and our environment. They form an energy ecology that can affect our feelings, our thoughts, and our overall well-being and vitality in both positive and negative ways.

Engaging with this ecology so that its effect on us and others is healthy, clear, life-giving, and positive is what energy hygiene is all about.

An Energy Body

Just as we have a physical body, we have an energy body as well. It receives impressions and vibrations from the surrounding energy ecology, and it radiates them out as well, reflecting the state of our own thinking and feeling. We are each a broadcasting and a receiving station combined.

Just as things you see and hear on the television can affect your emotions and your thoughts, so can these subtle energies as they engage with your energy body, though in a different way. We respond consciously to things we see and hear, but the energy body resonates with the energies and impulses it encounters. It becomes like them, like a chameleon changing its skin color to blend with its surroundings. This resonance is unconscious for most people though the effects are not. We may feel our thoughts and feelings are our own and not realize we may have picked up some of them through the interaction of our energy body with the subtle energies in our environment.

Psychic Lint

Generally speaking our energy body has its equivalent to our physical immune system and resists intrusion. But through resonance, it can pick up bits of subtle energies in much the way a sweater picks up lint. Depending on the nature of this "psychic lint" and the resonance it has with us, it can cling and influence us with its qualities and energy. Usually, it's a bit of mental or emotional information, saying "feel this emotion" or "think this thought." For example, if you go into a room filled with anxiety, you may not know consciously what has happened but your energy body senses and picks up the anxious energy in the room. Bits of "anxiety lint" attach, giving you the message, "Feel fear. Feel anxious." And this energy message, like any other stimulus from the environment, can pass into your unconscious mind and then into your consciousness. You find yourself feeling anxious but for no reason that you can detect.

We are all shedding such psychic lint into our environment all the time from our thoughts and feelings. Most of it dissipates and is transformed, but some of it persists and builds up, accumulating in certain places or around a person. It can be positive or negative in its effect. The home of a spiritual person can radiate with uplifting subtle energies, making us feel good the moment we cross the threshold. But the home of someone in the grips of depression may be filled with depressive thoughts and feelings that give the atmosphere of the place a gloomy feel even if the owner is not present.

In the normal course of our day, we may pick up and discard such lint many times. But sometimes it is not discarded. We carry it with us and it can begin to accumulate. Bits of subtle energy become stuck within our own energy body. When this happens, such a stuck place can become a "lint trap" attracting and holding to other bits of psychic lint that we may encounter. Energy hygiene is a way of clearing this stuff away and removing it so no one is affected adversely by it.

Energy Connections

In the physical world, we are separated by distance. What happens to someone on the far side of the earth may seem to have little consequence or affect upon me. We believe our thoughts and feelings are private, locked within our skulls and our skins. But in the energy world, we are all connected in profound and interdependent ways. It's as if we were all standing on a great trampoline. When one person bounces, it makes the whole trampoline move and we all bounce to some degree. Subtle energies are not limited by distance. Thus when a calamity strikes in some part of the world, our energy bodies all feel the effect of the suffering and fear no matter where we are. We may feel uneasy or restless, anxious or fearful for no reason we can see.

We live in turbulent, troubling times. The news is filled with one crisis after another from war and terrorism to economic turmoil to global climate change. People are afraid, and this fear is often intensified by public media. Through our technological ability to communicate images, thoughts, and feelings quickly and dramatically, we have developed ways of blowing our psychic lint—particularly our fears, anxieties, angers, hatreds, and pessimism—around the world so that it affects all of us. Where in previous centuries, such subtle psychic lint would have dissipated and transformed, now it is repeated, reinforced, and strengthened by global media and our subtle energy connections until it accumulates in our world, no longer just "lint" but true psychic pollution weighing upon all of us.

More Than Protection

Energy hygiene is a procedure for dealing with psychic lint and psychic pollution. It is a way of working with subtle energies to create a clear, clean, positive, vibrant and healthy energy environment both within ourselves and in our immediate environment. When we use these procedures to deal with larger issues of psychic pollution in the world, then it becomes subtle activism, which is simply energy hygiene for the planet at large.

Good physical hygiene is about more than taking a shower or keeping clean; it's about all that we do to ensure the health and optimal function of our body. The same is true with energy hygiene. There are techniques of "lint removal" that can be learned and also ways of protecting ourselves to keep the psychic lint off in the first place. But energy hygiene is much more than just a defensive or cleansing process. It's about vitalizing and expressing a healthy wholeness of spirit, mind, heart, and body. It's about honoring and nourishing sovereignty, identity, coherency, and boundaries on the one hand and developing and practicing connectedness, engagement, love, and a compassionate participation in life on the other. Energy hygiene is the expression of an incarnational spirituality.

Three Rules of Energy Hygiene

There are three rules of good energy hygiene. They are:
1. Flow
2. Positivity
3. Connectedness

Each of us is like a pool of energy. As long as energy is flowing in and out in a healthy way, this pool is alive, clear and clean; when this flow is obstructed by a buildup of psychic lint, then the pool can begin to stagnate. Restoring and maintaining a healthy flow of energy is important. A good walk, physical activity, learning something new, doing something kind for someone else are all simple ways of restoring flow; there are also techniques for restoring this flow on a subtle energy level. The exercise included here is one example of such a technique.

Being positive is more than just practicing positive thinking, though that can be helpful. Positivity is a condition of being radiant, open, giving, confident, and strong. It is an energy state as much as a psychological one. There are many ways of developing and maintaining this state, but they are all enhanced by valuing and honoring yourself and standing in your uniqueness and sovereignty.

Connectedness opens us to a larger world beyond ourselves and enables us to participate in a greater wholeness. Just as a pool stagnates that is unconnected to living streams of water and ultimately to the ocean on the one hand and the wellsprings deep within the earth on the other, so we need to be connected to the vitality and life, the spirit and wellbeing of the world around us. We create good energy conditions for ourselves not by isolating ourselves behind shields and barriers but by creating good energy in the world around us. Compassionately and lovingly participating in the life of our world and contributing to the wellbeing of all life is a vital part of energy hygiene.

II. SUBTLE ACTIVISM

Subtle activism is a procedure for dealing with imbalanced subtle energies within the world. The imbalance may have come from physical events or activities, such as the impact of a natural disaster upon a human community. Or it may have arisen out of human psychological states, such as fear or hatred. Subtle activism can also be used to reinforce and enhance the flow of positive and creative energies in the world. It is not just a way of dealing with problems.

Subtle activism is a way of working with your own incarnational presence and spiritual resources to create a clear, clean, positive, vibrant and healthy energy environment. When this procedure is used to deal with psychic pollution within and around yourself, then it becomes energy hygiene. Energy hygiene is simply subtle activism at a personal level.

Not a Substitute

Subtle activism is not a substitute for taking action and doing good in wise and compassionate ways in the physical world. Physical activism is necessary for we live in a world where pain and suffering, hunger and disease, oppression and injustice, pollution and environmental degradation have real physical manifestations and consequences. Subtle activism is not instead of but in addition to work and effort to heal the world and ourselves.

However, because it's invisible to most people, the subtle energy world can go underestimated and ignored. Yet its effects when negative can hinder and diminish outer efforts at helping in the world and even create or intensify imbalance and negativity in the world. Conversely, when positive its effects can support and enhance the good efforts of physical activists to relieve suffering and injustice.

Subtle activism is not a substitute but it is an important complement to outer activism. More importantly, in many cases when the cause of suffering and imbalance originates or is perpetuated in the energy realm, it may be the only form of activism that can effectively make a difference.

More than Cleansing or Fixing

Subtle activism is also much more than just a process of rescuing, fixing, or cleansing. It's about creating, vitalizing and expressing wholeness. It's about honoring and nourishing sovereignty, identity, coherency, and boundaries on the one hand and developing and practicing connectedness, engagement, love, and a compassionate participation in life on the other. In its full expression, it's a practice of "walking whole" and enhancing the wholeness and incarnation of Gaia.

Although the idea of doing subtle activism comes up most frequently in relationship to troubles in the world, it can also be used as a way to support and bless good actions or promising situations. A laboratory where researchers are working on a cancer cure, a diplomatic meeting where statesmen are trying to work out a just relationship between nations, a school where teachers are trying to give students the best education they can are all examples of situations and conditions that can be the subject for supportive subtle activism.

Seven Rules of Subtle Activism

Here are seven basic rules of good subtle activism.

1. Don't Impose. We each have our own personal energies, our own opinions and ideas about how the world should be and how people should live for their highest good. We resent it when someone else tries to impose their way of being, thinking, and doing upon us, particularly if it's very different from our own. When we are in trouble, we may need help, but we resist being thought of as something to be "fixed." We want and need help in a form that honors and respects our own sovereignty, that empowers us to develop our own capacities, that helps us to grow, and enables us as much as possible to find our own solutions to the problems. We want assistance but we want empowerment as well.

This is true in any situation. The subtle activist doesn't seek to impose his or her "way" or energies upon a situation but seeks to create openness for the innate spirit, health, and wisdom within people to emerge and express in a manner unique to them and appropriate to the situation.

2. Partnering with the "Stakeholders." With this in mind, a subtle activist wants to identify the "stakeholders" in the situation, that is, who is being affected or will be affected by the outcomes of the situation. In doing inner work, he or she wants to connect and collaborate energetically with the spirit of those involved, or at least be aware that the work is done on their behalf. This also helps the subtle activist remember that the work is one of partnership with the people involved and not one of acting alone.

3. Be Connected to Higher Powers and Allies. Dealing with the psychic pollution and negative subtle energies of the world is not something any person can do on his or her own, any more than one person could clear away all the rubble and rescue all the survivors in a town devastated by an earthquake. We need allies. We need to be connected to the larger spirit of wholeness in the earth, which I am calling Gaia. We need to be aligned and connected with the Sacred. If we don't have any physical allies to work with, we can seek out allies of a spiritual nature who themselves live and work within the realms of subtle energy. And as I said, we need to work with the souls and energies of those whom we seek to help.

4. Stay Grounded and Aligned. In this process we want to be sure that we are grounded. I mean this in three ways. We want to be grounded in our own identity and personhood, feeling whole and good about ourselves. We don't want to bring our inner conflicts into our subtle activism. This is the first leg of attunement to sovereignty and our own incarnational wholeness.

We want to be energetically grounded in our immediate, local environment, our subtle energy connected to and anchored in the energy fields around us: in the earth, in the things around us, the nature around us, and so forth. This is the function of Grail Space.

Finally, we want to be grounded in and aligned with Gaia, the spirit of wholeness and incarnation within the world. This ensures that we will be sensitive to and act on behalf of the wholeness and integration of a situation and not just for the immediate goals of some faction within that situation. We are acting as agents of the whole earth, not just of human interests or of some particular group within humanity.

5. Be Inclusive, Seeing the Sacredness in All Involved. Of course, implicit in this as I said earlier is an attunement to the Sacred, to the Ground of All Being. Sometimes, a person drawn to subtle activism sees himself or herself as a "warrior of Light" going forth to do battle with "forces of darkness." It's easy to frame a situation so that there are "friends" to help and "enemies" to combat. But subtle activism is not spiritual combat. It is an act of healing, which is inclusive by its nature. There are no enemies in subtle activism, only conditions to be understood, held in love and positive energies, and transformed. When we are aligned with sacredness, we feel this inclusiveness more powerfully.

6. Honor the Specific and the Particular. Attuning to the Sacred is for most of us akin to attuning to the universal and the transpersonal. But we want to be attuned to the specific as well, to the particular conditions that define the situation for which we are doing subtle activism. Such a situation involves specific people in a specific place meeting specific challenges which will have specific consequences. Our work as subtle activists is to bring the wholeness and spirit of the universal into connection and engagement with all these specificities. We need to honor the specific.

7. Embody and Be What You "Send." One way we honor the specific is to embody in ourselves the spirit and energy that we wish to bring to the situation or the outcome that we would like to help promote. If it is a situation of conflict, for instance, then we want to embody peacefulness, calm, and the wisdom to resolve that conflict. We don't simply "project" peace and hope (or insist) that whoever is involved picks up on that quality and embodies it; we're not telling others "you must be peaceful." Instead, we embody these qualities in the specificity of our own being and place ourselves energetically in the situation where we can be an energetic presence around which the subtle energies of that environment can configure. We must be whatever it is that we "send."

There are many techniques of subtle activism, many different ways in which individuals and groups can participate in this endeavor. But at its core, subtle activism is a process of creating wholeness. These rules of not imposing, partnering the stakeholders, being grounded, forming connections, being collaborative, being inclusive, and honoring the specific are all simply ways of doing so.

III. COLLABORATIVE MIND

If you've ever been with someone, even if you're not having a conversation, and find yourself sparking with ideas and inspiration as if your thinking has kicked into a higher gear, you've experienced collaborative mind: the joining of two mental fields into a symbiotic, mutually enhancing holism. This can happen in complete silence as the product of a shared companionship. It's not telepathy necessarily. It's not that you and others are exchanging thoughts, though that might happen, too. Rather it's that your own private powers of thought and feeling are enhanced, brought into a larger space that is co-created in subtle ways by the interaction of your presence with that of others.

We are familiar with the idea of collaborative thinking, expressed in the axiom "two heads are better than one." It is part of the art of brainstorming in which two or more people share thoughts and ideas to create a field in which new perspectives and insights can emerge. Collaborative Presence is a deeper expression of that. It's not so much that you are being stimulated by other thoughts as it is that your own mental and emotional space and even your very incarnational presence is enlarged and made more spacious.

Rather than two glasses clinking together, it's like two glasses merging so that a larger glass which can hold more liquid results. This sense of greater area and spaciousness is the phenomenon of collaborative mind.

If we are working with an inner ally, this being is not providing information or guidance or data per se but is aligning its mental energy with ours so that our own mind is heightened or brightened or expanded or made more spacious. Our thinking is enhanced. In my own experience, this has been the primary way in which beings from the subtle worlds have interacted with me. Our mutual presences are enhanced in what I think of as an alliance space. In effect, we are expressing a collaborative presence.

To me, this is the main function for inner world contact. If we think just of getting guidance or advice or having a conversation, we can separate ourselves into us and them, ourselves and the ally. It can become a transactional relationship. But collaborative presence is like a gifting relationship, a giving of oneself to the other in full sovereignty so that both are enhanced. And isn't that what an alliance is about? Because inner beings are, by our standards, beings of subtle energy, they can interact directly with our mental and emotional energy fields. Their presence can help expand those fields. The result is a feeling of greater spaciousness, energy, presence and expanded possibility in our thinking.

Collaborative presence adds powerfully to our work with energy hygiene and subtle activism. And in this context, our attunement and alignment to Gaia is itself a form of collaborative presence, one that enhances our ability to render blessing to the world.

Allies

In the work of energy hygiene and subtle activism, all one really needs is the "three-legged stool" of attunement to self anchored in an attunement to your immediate environment and enhanced by attunement to Gaia. These three can create a powerful field of presence that can have an effect on the subtle half of the earth and act as a lens through which the Light of sacredness can shine.

However, it's possible to add a fourth leg to the stool, and that is the presence of non-physical allies. Human beings have been reaching out to spiritual allies for millennia; it is one of the oldest and most natural ways in which people have engaged with earth's subtle half. Such allies can be animal spirits, nature spirits, ancestors, human teachers working from the spiritual realms, guardian spirits, devas and angels, just to name a few. People reach out to such allies for assistance, guidance, instruction, knowledge, inspiration, companionship, protection, healing, and blessing

In the context of Incarnational Spirituality, the beings of the subtle worlds are citizens of the world as much as we who live in the physical universe; ultimately it's only by acting together that the world can manifest its wholeness and unfold its fullest potentials of life. We need to develop a partnership cosmology.

Throughout the centuries people have developed many ways of contacting and working with subtle beings. These range from actions as simple as prayer to complex magical and religious rituals. Behind all these actions is an acknowledgement that earth's subtle half is different, in some cases profoundly different, from the familiar physical world. Sometimes this difference inspires awe, sometimes fear, and sometimes incredulity, suspicion and outright disbelief and dismissal. While interaction across the boundary between the two halves of the world can be as natural and as close as dreaming, successful deliberate, mindful interaction requires sensitivity and discernment.

At the heart of this interaction is the concept of alliance. In a way, we have already been studying this idea. Sovereignty and the potency of one's own incarnational field arise from seeing one's soul, one's personality, and one's body as allies. Grail Space is about seeing the things around you in your local environment as allies. The Gaian relationship is about seeing the world as an ally.

In an alliance, all partners are equally honored and respected; each is seen as necessary to the success and wholeness of the alliance. This does not mean that the partners are equal in power, energy, knowledge, wisdom, status, or resources. An alliance between the United States and Switzerland is not a partnership between two countries of equal power in the world. But in the context of the alliance, both countries contribute something that the other wants or needs; in the context of the alliance, both are equal partners.

It's important to understand this principle when working with the subtle worlds. In the earth's subtle half are beings whose consciousnesses are much vaster and more complex than our own; they have power beyond our own, at least in their own sphere of activity. There are also beings who are much less than we, not nearly as developed or evolved; our powers are far beyond their own. Yet in true alliance, these differences enhance the partnership and are held in a context of mutual esteem, love, and respect.

The "three-legged stool" of attunement to self, environment and Gaia can be seen as a practice in creating alliances. It establishes an alliance field which can be a foundation for contacting and creating an alliance with a subtle being.

There are many ways for doing this, as I said above. The alliance field is not so much a technique as it is an attitude. It's a way of relating.

On occasion I give lectures to people at a far distance from where I live using Skype or some similar computer-based electronic technology. Without this technology, I would not be able to see and hear the group that I am working with. But my relationship with that group—the way that I relate to them—is independent of that technology. Whether a person is face to face before me or on the other side of the world and we are communicating through telephone or computer, I still want to engage with that person in a respectful, honoring and loving way. And I want to do so from a position of honoring and respecting myself as well. A technique may make the communication possible but the relationship itself is rooted in my heart and mind and in how lovingly I can hold the other.

This is true for working with subtle beings. Because they inhabit dimensions quite different from the physical world, one that is generally out of the range of perception for my physical senses, I need some way of connecting with them that is different from what I use to see the material world around me. There are many such ways. But once the connection is made, the nature of the engagement obeys the same principles for good relationships that guide my conduct and awareness in the physical world.

When I talk with a clerk in a store, for instance, I can honor this person and pay attention to him or to her, but I don't worship him or her or necessarily believe everything he or she tells me. I use my own wisdom and discernment to evaluate what is said, and I make my own sovereign choices as to what I will accept or act upon. The same is true in dealing with the subtle worlds. Because a being has no physical form and may be energetically more impressive and powerful than I am is no reason to surrender my sovereignty and integrity. An alliance doesn't demand or require that kind of surrender; it only asks that we respect and listen to each other as partners.

In working with the subtle half of the world, one principle is important to keep in mind. The effect of the contact needs to honor and assist our incarnations, not make them less capable, less integrated, and less coherent. If any contact seems to make us less able to function effectively and well in our everyday lives, it needs to be reevaluated and if necessary stopped. If our ability to add to the world's coherency and wholeness is diminished—if, for example, an inner contact has the result of making us more selfish or arrogant, filling us with a feeling of being special so that we cannot properly honor, love and empower those around us—then that contact, at least in the form in which we are experiencing or interpreting it, is disrupting our overall incarnational integrity. We are becoming less whole, not more so.

Incarnational spirituality offers some specific procedures and tools for contacting and working with the subtle worlds and with non-physical allies, but these all depend on our facility in constructing our three-legged stool. And in the end, no technique, no matter how sophisticated, can substitute for a wise, discerning and loving heart and mind.

EXERCISES FOR CHAPTER FIVE

ENERGY HYGIENE

Basic Energy Hygiene Exercise

The first fundamental element of energy hygiene—and of good energy health—is flow. The second fundamental element is that this flow is positive, life-giving, and that it creates wholeness both within oneself and for others. The third fundamental element is connectedness with Gaia and the core of life that is the Generative Mystery, the Sacred.

Here is a very simple exercise to get flow going again:

1. Make a Connection: Reach out and touch something. Feel its texture and nature under your fingers. Let your attention flow towards the object you're touching. Appreciate it for what it is.

2. Expand your Heart: Think of a happy memory or pleasurable moment, something that gives you an inner sense of expansion, and draw that memory into your heart where you can feel it as a warm glow within you. Allow this glow to expand.

3. Send Love through your Connection: Direct the feeling of this expanding glow out from your heart, down your arm and into your fingers and into the object you're touching. Feel love develop for the object you're touching. Pause to appreciate the relationship and flow you have with this object.

4. Connect to Gaia: Be aware that you are standing within a vast, living world, one filled with abundant, flowing energy and love. Let the feeling of spaciousness surround you and fill you. Imagine the whole world embraced and held by a loving presence. Feel the love of this presence flowing into your expanded, glowing heart and down your arm and your hand and your fingers into the object you are touching. Feel yourself and this object expanding as this

spaciousness flows into and around you.

5. Connect to Environment: Let this flow of spacious energy and love flowing from Gaia through your heart and into the object you're touching now flow out from that object into the environment around you. As it does so, you find yourself and your energy field bathed and participating in a flow of energy from Gaia and the sacredness within it through you and around you into and through the object you're touching and into the environment.

6. Complete the Circuit: See the flow of spacious, loving energy rising from your environment back into Gaia, back into the sacred, completing the circuit. Just feel the energy of this flow moving through and around you, bathing you, bathing your environment; it's a current flowing from the sacred into Gaia, into you, through you, out from you and into the environment through the object you're touching, and back into Gaia, back into the sacred.

7. Hold your Energy: As you stand in this flowing circuit, hold yourself and your energy field, along with whatever fears, negativity, or stuckness you were experiencing, in this flow, like holding dirty clothes under a rushing stream. You don't have to do anything except release your energy field to be filled, cleared, cleansed, and blessed.

8. Complete. When you feel complete, let go of the object you were touching, breaking the circuit. Invite and allow the sense of connection to a larger, more spacious whole and the sense of your own energy flowing and circulating to integrate gracefully into your body and into your life. Your flow restored, go about your daily activities.

Energy Hygiene Using Grail Space

The Grail Space exercise is designed to bless and energize a room or an environment by calling forth its deeper, foundational energies of identity and sacredness. It's not specifically an energy hygiene practice, though it does evoke the "self-cleaning" and self-clearing potentialities of a place.

Here is version that brings it in line with our energy hygiene discussion. This is designed to be done in a human space, like a building or room. It can be adapted to be used outdoors simply by leaving out the architectural elements such as floors and walls and changing furniture references to items found in the natural environment where you may be doing this exercise.

1. Stand in your own sovereignty, attuning to your own self-light, your individuality, your soul, your innate sacredness.

2. Attune to and evoke the Grail Space of your environment as per the Grail Space Exercise.

3. Attune to Gaia, the spirit of life and wholeness within the world and thus within your immediate environment.

4. From the inner space of these attunements, call forth to the sacredness within your environment, from the land beneath you, from the floor beneath you, from any rug upon the floor, from the walls around you, from the ceiling above you.

5. Call forth to the sacredness from the furniture about you, from any decorations or art work around you, from any and all items and objects that are around you.

6. Let this sacredness pour into the Grail Space of the room or environment as well as into yourself. Feel its blessing and energy. This energy aligns everything within the room to its liberated and original identity, to its essential will-to-be, to the life and sacredness within it, to the wholeness and integrity within it and to its connectedness to the cosmos as a whole.

7. This energy holds in light and love any held, trapped or

stuck energies that do not belong in this space, that do not add to the sacredness and wellbeing of this place, that do not integrate with or honor the identity of this place and all within it, that do not contribute to wholeness and the blessing of all beings and all life, or that obstruct or prohibit the free circulation of living, renewing energies that connect this place and all within it to the wholeness of life and the sacredness within that wholeness. As these energies are held, they are released, transmuted, dissolved, or removed, liberated to continue on their own journey into sacredness, liberated to return to the flow and circulation of energies that support and bless all life.

8. Hold this Grail Space and its transforming, transmuting, blessing Light as long as feels comfortable to you. When you feel complete, draw your own Grail Space back into your Incarnational Field, into your self-light and sovereignty, and into your body, letting the Light within the room or environment assimilate as it will into you and your surroundings. Go forth into your normal activities.

SUBTLE ACTIVISM:
THE BASIC PROCESS WITH EXAMPLE

Here is a description of one process you can use to do Subtle Activism. I'm focusing it upon the situation in Japan following the earthquake, tsunami and nuclear plant disaster. I'm breaking it down into four simple steps:

1. Preparation
2. Connection
3. Holding
4. Completion

Preparation

The first thing you do is gather your energy into an integrated, coherent field organized around your intent. Here are the basic things you wish to do, though the order in which you do them and how you do them is up to you.

— Be clear about your intent. What are you seeking to accomplish with this act of energy activism?

— Attune to your own unique incarnational energy, your sense of your inner strength, light, peace, love, and sovereignty.

— Attune to where you are, to your immediate environment in which you will do this work. Bless and honor this environment and thank it for its assistance. It is the "cup" that holds you while you work and you can draw energy from it.

— Attune to Gaia, the spirit of wholeness, balance, and life within the world.

Connection

In this step, you are connecting to any specific allies on the one hand and to your "target," the person, people, condition, place, or situation on behalf of whom you are doing the energy activism.

1. As an example, let us make the target the area of devastation in northern Japan resulting from the earthquake and tsunami of March 11, 2011.

2. Here the primary ally is the Angel of Japan, or if you wish, the Soul of the Japanese people. This is the Being who holds in its love and presence the destiny, the wellbeing, the evolution, and the wholeness of Japan and its inhabitants, as well as its contribution to all humanity and to the world. Imagine this Being and connect to it, seeing your field, gathered in the Preparation Stage, connecting to the field of this Being. Imagine both fields interacting and supporting each other and creating together like a soap bubble emerging from between you a shared field of intentional, healing, transformative, loving energy.

3. Now imagine your "target" and its field. Connect the joint field, the bubble created by you and the Soul of Japan, with the area of devastation and suffering as a result of the triple disasters in recent days. This area is filled with its own inner helpers, nature spirits, ancestors, allies of one kind or another, as well as the physical human beings. Imagine all these being united in a single energy field.

4. You are not forcing or injecting or pushing your joint field upon this local, united field within the devastated areas. You are not imposing. Rather you are inviting it to join with you so that a larger joint "bubble" now emerges, a field shared by all of you.

5. Connect this joint bubble with Gaia and the Sacred. Your "bubble" of work is held by this larger Source so that it can be a blessing for all involved.

Holding

In this step you are doing the actual work of the subtle activism. The joint field you have created, held in the spirit and love of Gaia and the Sacred, becomes the place within which energies can be healed, engaged, transformed, alchemized, clarified, freed, blessed, and so forth.

1. In this joint field, state the intent you have for this act of subtle activism. State what you wish to accomplish, the healing you think should take place, or the transformation or liberation of energies and conditions, or whatever it may be. Offer the energy of your intent and ask your partners--the Soul of Japan and the spirit of the devastated area--to do the same. Remember, you are not seeking to impose your will; you are seeking to create a shared field in which a will can emerge that will bless all concerned and fulfill the deepest intents that all the parties have. But in this process, you have every right to state your intent as a contribution to the whole.

2. Hold this energy field to give it a chance to attune as well to the intent of the Soul of Japan and the will of the spiritual forces

acting in the devastated area.

3. Hold this joint energy field until you feel tired or restless or feel complete.

Completion

At this point you bring this operation to a close.

1. Release the energy field of the devastated area, seeking it held within the larger wholeness of the sacredness within Gaia that has held all of you. Give thanks to all involved

2. Release the energy field of your ally, the Soul of Japan. Give thanks for its participation and help.

3. Let your own energy field gracefully integrate into your sovereignty and your body and into your surroundings. Give thanks to both for their assistance. Go about your normal activity when you are ready.

MASSAGING THE WORLD: A Subtle Activism Exercise

This is a simple exercise in Subtle Activism. In thinking about what you are doing here, imagine that you are a body worker about to give a massage. The actual pain that the client is experiencing is deep within the body, out of reach ad beyond your ability to reach it directly. But by working with the muscles and tissues that are available to you, you set a relaxing, healing force to work within the body as a whole.

This exercise operates on the premise that like the body, the world is a whole system in which every part is connected to every other part. By working on one layer, deeper layers can be affected in positive ways. By working on what is at hand, conditions that are distant can be affected as well, particularly if those distant or deeper areas are held in mind and the connections affirmed.

1. Begin by putting yourself into as loving a mood as possible, centering that love in your heart. You might do this by remembering or imagining people and places that you love. Allow that love to fill your heart until it becomes a flame ablaze with a compassionate and loving fire. If you wish, connect with the Sacred and allow its love and compassion to join with yours.

2. Feel and see this love moving out from your heart, down your arms and into your hands and fingers. Feel your fingers begin to glow and radiate with this love. As you do so, ask that this love become a force for healing, balance and wholeness.

3. Put your hands on something in your environment that is touching a floor or the earth. If you can put your hand on the earth directly this is preferable, but it is not necessary. Just visualize the connections that exist between whatever you are touching and the earth as a whole.

4. If you wish, let your fingers move upon whatever you are touching, just as if you were massaging it. You want to feel fingers of energy and love moving deeper to touch and massage the energetic field of whatever you are touching. As you do, let your attention be upon letting your energy serve and bless the energy and presence of whatever you are touching and through it, the larger energy field of your immediate environment. Allow yourself to come into a loving and blessing connection with the energy field of your immediate environment. At this stage, you are not trying to do anything more than bless and "massage" the energy that is around you, the world you immediately inhabit.

5. As you feel a state of integration and harmony and flow develop between you and your environment, call to mind a situation in the world that you would like to serve and to which you wish to offer an energy of love, healing, peace, and blessing. Continue to extend a healing, calming, blessing energy into your environment, but now imagine the lines of connection between where you are and

the distant place you wish to bless. Don't try to "go" there in your imagination. Keep yourself focused on blessing and serving what you can immediately touch, the environment around you. But just know that through the medium of a deeper Intelligence within the body of the earth, your intent to heal and bless will be received and honored in places where it is needed but which you cannot reach directly in any physical way.

6. When you feel tired or restless or have a sense of completion, just remove your hands. Sit for a moment and let the energy of love and spirit circulate through your body, relaxing and empowering you and filling you with grace. Then give thanks, and go about your daily affairs.

WEBMAKING: A Subtle Activism Exercise

Overview

Here is another very simple form of subtle activism which can be performed anywhere at any time. I call it Webmaking as you are contributing to a web of Light. The overall intent is similar to that of the exercise I just presented, but the approach is different.

The brain has been discovered to be "plastic," always changing in dynamic ways as we respond and adapt to our environment. In the developing science of neuroplasticity, it has been demonstrated that the twin powers of intention and attention when directed in certain ways can result in lasting changes in brain structure. As we change our brain structure, so we change our behavior and our capacities. In other words, the power of thinking can have a more profound physical effect than science had previously suspected.

There is a similar phenomenon at work in the non-physical or subtle environment of the world, the environment in which subtle activism takes place. We are constantly forming energetic connections between ourselves and others and between ourselves and our surroundings. Even simple acts of perception and recognition can do this. The quality and nature of these connections depend on the kind of subtle energies we weave into them. If they are negative in nature, it results in one kind of subtle connection and structure; if they are positive, it results in a different one. Further, the intensity and intentionality behind our thinking and feeling determines how long these connections and this subtle structure may last. Most dissolve immediately as our attention shifts and moves about, but some can persist and eventually stabilize into a long-lasting configuration of subtle energies.

One of the tasks of subtle activism is to shift the subtle structure of the world away from being stuck in violent, hateful and negative configurations towards patterns and flows of energy that are healthy, holistic, loving, caring, and nurturing. It is a work of generating a structure, a "web" of positive qualities and energies that can support and bless individuals, attune them to the loving inclusiveness of the Sacred, and foster goodwill and collaborative behavior that creates wholeness in the world. If this is done on a regular basis, then patterns develop that persist within the subtle world.

This exercise is something we can do "on the run," as we go about our daily lives. Think of a spider spinning a web. It anchors a strand of silk on something solid and then swings out to connect with something else where it attaches the other end of that strand. In Webmaking, you are making a connection between an individual and the Sacred, a connection that is a strand of blessing.

As I said earlier, when I use the term "Sacred," I don't mean any particular religious image of God, though you can certainly use whatever image of deity is important to you and in which you believe. What I mean is a universal Ground of All Being, which seeks to bless each individual life according to its uniqueness and its needs, enabling it to fulfill in optimal ways its potentials.

Webmaking is something you do with anyone you meet during your day. As per the rules of subtle activism, you are not imposing anything, nor are you projecting a particular energy to anyone. You are, however, establishing a connection of a particular nature—the strand of the web. You can even do this with objects in your environment and certainly with animals and plants as well. This web of Light and lovingness ultimately connects all to all.

We could say that there already is a universal Web—the Sacred itself—that connects everything to everything else, and we would be right. But operationally in our lives and in the life of the earth this universal Web is often more potential than realized. We have but to watch the evening news to see how fully and tragically humanity falls short of implementing it. Further, the activities of disconnection and violence, fear and anger in which humanity does participate creates a very different kind of subtle energy structure, one that breaks the sacred Web and prevents it from manifesting. Our collective "brain" is badly wired, creating habits of separation and violence that only make that faulty wiring more persistent.

The good news is that the subtle environment, like our brain, is very plastic and can change, often very quickly. We can create inner structures and configurations of energy that support and promote wholeness. What is needed for this to happen, though, is for us to make those changes through the power of our intentionality and our attention. We have to intend goodwill, intend love, intend collaboration, intend understanding and then we must give those intentions our attention and focus, particularly where those qualities don't exist or are being undermined in a given situation. So while the universal Web of connection, life and love is there, we can't simply take it for granted. It's up to us to participate in its expression and to do what we can to manifest it.

In Webmaking, then, there are three steps in doing this. The first step is to make a connection with another individual, to "spin a strand" in his or her direction. The second step is to connect that strand to the Sacred. The third step is to further connect that strand to a larger, evolving web that you are part of co-creating. Let's look at each of these in more detail with some examples.

The Exercise:

Part 1: Spinning a Strand

When you see an individual—it doesn't matter whether you know them or not—imagine a ribbon or strand of Light between you and that person. This strand is NOT tying or binding you two together in anyway; it is simply a carrier of your goodwill, love, and blessings to that person. In effect, you are affirming a universal truth: "We are connected in the love and blessings of the Sacred; we are connected in the universal web of life that seeks to manifest wholeness on the earth. Between us there is no violence or separation, only goodwill and mutual support." With your strand, you are activating and expressing this truth.

You can do this with anyone. For example, while driving, you can spin strands to other drivers around you. While shopping, you can spin a strand to other shoppers or to the clerks that serve you. In a restaurant, you can spin a strand to other diners and to the waitpersons who bring you your food. And you can spin strands to plants, animals and objects as well. The possibilities are endless.

Part 2: Connecting to the Sacred

Imagine this strand of light and blessing that you've spun between yourself and another and extend it beyond yourself into the Sacred, however you imagine that Presence. This is important. You are spinning the strand, not anchoring it in yourself. You are anchoring it in the Sacred, in the Beloved of All Beings, the Ground of all existence. This prevents unwanted psychic links from coming into being between you and another, assuming that the link lasted anytime at all. The Sacred is the universal anchor for the web of life.

If this is the case, why have the first step at all? Why not directly see the individual as connected to the Sacred and leave out yourself as a middle person? There are several reasons. For one, there is a benefit to your personal expression of caring and goodwill; this is good for you and it's good for the recipient. For another, you and the other individual (or plant, animal or object) have a natural resonance already by virtue of being part of this physical world. You can form a connection along this natural resonance that then becomes a "carrier wave" for the deeper connection with the Sacred. You provide the specific connection that then can be connected to the Universal.

It's not that you don't wish to acknowledge or empower your

connectedness to the other; it's that you don't want to anchor that connectedness in yourself. Once the connection is recognized and affirmed through your intentionality and attention, you then want its "end point" to be established within a larger, universal field that embraces both of you. That larger field is the Sacred.

Part 3: Connecting to a web

The next time you "spin a strand" of light and blessing between yourself and another and connect it to the Sacred, think back to the previous such strands you've "spun." Visualize this new strand connecting to them, forming a web. See this web filled with the Light of the Sacred and vibrating to its loving and supportive presence. You don't have to remember each separate strand, each connection you've made as you've gone through your day but do remember and visualize the wholeness of the growing web itself. See this web that you're spinning as connected to and reflecting the universal Web that is the underlying wholeness and life within all things.

In performing these three steps, don't forget that you have a personal strand yourself between yourself and the Sacred. Be sure to think of this from time to time to renew your own connections and participation in the larger Web.

Afterword to webmaking: Intention and Attention

What makes this exercise work is the intention behind the Webmaking and the attention you bring to it. Each strand you spin and send out to connect a person to the universal Web needs to have your clear and clean intention behind it. Part of that intention is your intent that that person (or animal, plant, or object) be blessed and, through connection with the Sacred, empowered in the expression of his, her, or its unique identity and soul's purpose. It is an intention of goodwill and love made impersonally and in a way that places no binding on the individual, no imposition upon his or her freedom, sovereignty and personal energy. You are not insisting that something happen. You are only augmenting the will of his or her soul and innate sacredness to unfold the highest of which he or she is capable.

To give power to this intention, you must then give attention to that person. This can be very brief, no more than a few seconds, but in that moment—however short—your whole attention is on that person and their wellbeing and connectedness to wholeness.

In short, in Webmaking, you have to mean it. It's not something you do idly or wishfully. It need not take much time or energy, only a second or two, but it needs to be sincere. For the three steps to work there needs to be intention and attention behind them.

If you practice this, you will find, however, that the growing strength and vitality of the web you're creating and its attunement to the universal Web will empower your ability to spin your strands. A deeper part of you, knowing what you intend and that you're sincere in following through, will take over and greatly augment the process, so it becomes almost automatic for you (though never taken for granted).

In this way, you become an agent for shaping the subtle environment of the world, drawing into manifestation the energies and patterns of the universal Web of wholeness. This is a powerful act of subtle activism. It means that when the individuals whose connections to that universal Web you have empowered encounter situations that may cause them to react in a negative way, they have something positive and life-affirming to respond to other than the habits of mental, emotional and physical violence engraved into the subtle fields of the earth. The function of all subtle activism is to bring new options into play and create loving alternatives to habitual action. That is what your Webmaking can help bring about.

COLLABORATIVE MIND

Collaborative Mind Exercise

The object of this exercise is not specifically to come to an insight or a resolution around some particular topic but rather to experience and explore the felt sense of being in an expanded mental field or having a felt sense of collaborative mind.

1. Pick a topic. I would suggest something that has energy and life for you, not simply an abstract idea like "butterfly hunting in the Himalayas". It could be an issue that you're dealing with or a decision you're thinking about.

2. Get into the mood by thinking about your topic, reviewing it and getting the flavor and energy of it.

3. Standing in your sovereignty, imagine yourself entering an open space dedicated to study, thought, learning, insight, and so forth. You might picture this as a library or a research center. Make sure this space feels comfortable and congenial to you.

4. Think about your topic while being in this space. How does this change the quality of your thinking, if at all?

5. Extend your awareness to see if you detect any others sharing this space with you, joining with you in the act of thinking. In other words, are there any others in the library with you? Feel the power and felt sense of shared thinking, of the presence of thinking happening.

6. Declare your topic. Hold the energy and felt sense of it in your mind. Ask if there are any in this field or space that, having your best interests at heart, would share in your thinking and link their minds to yours to think together about this topic. You are asking for the creation of a shared mental field to support the act of thinking itself, particularly with respect to your topic.

7. Pay attention to any sensations or energies you may feel, any change in your felt sense of this space or in your experience of your own thinking.

8. Go ahead and continue thinking about your topic but now with an underlying awareness or felt sense that you are not alone in your thinking about it. Can you feel any expanded field of thinking within you or around you? Do you feel any change in how you are

thinking and processing your topic?

9. Continue thinking until you feel some insight, resolution, or feel the energy is waning, your thoughts are scattering, or there is some other indication that the session is finished. Take a moment to review your experience, in particular the felt sense of being in an expanded mental field. Did anything happen? What was this field like, if you experienced it? If you didn't experience it, did anything seem to block it?

An introduction to

Chapter Six: Practicing Incarnational Spirituality

The application of Incarnational Spirituality is as varied as the individuals who practice it. It could hardly be otherwise since each incarnation is a unique relationship between a person and the world. It is up to each of us to determine how our individual expression of this relationship may best unfold with blessings to ourselves and to the world around us.   In this sense, the practice of Incarnational Spirituality is very much a matter of personal crafting, discovering what works for us in the particular circumstances of our lives. This is in keeping with one of the basic elements of Incarnational Spirituality which is an appreciation and honoring of our individuality.

But this doesn't mean there are no suggestions for an incarnational spiritual practice that may be shared by all of us. In this final chapter, I offer some ideas for elements that such a practice may include.

Going to "L"

An incarnation is an interaction and relationship between two very different states of being and consciousness. We commonly call these two the spiritual and physical realms and the soul and the personality. Incarnational Spirituality is the study of this relationship and how these two different states intersect and blend and how they can hold each other creatively so that each can offer its unique contributions without being overwhelmed by the other. The keyword here is wholeness.

For this reason, any Incarnational Spirituality practice will generally have three elements: one that deals with the vertical side of the relationship, the interaction with spirit and soul; one that deals with the horizontal side of the relationship, the interaction with the physical world and the personality; and one that deals with their interaction and integration.

We may picture these elements as represented by the letter "L" with its vertical and horizontal arms.

115

These three elements can be approached in a wide variety of ways. The vertical "arm" is traditionally the arena of spirituality with a focus on attunement to the Sacred, to the transpersonal, and to the spiritual worlds. The horizontal "arm" is traditionally the area of self-development, psychology, medicine, economics, politics, and all those disciplines that deal with our physical nature and our interactions with each other and with the world. But Incarnational Spirituality is more than a contemplative or mystical discipline and more than the practice of self-help and personal development. It includes these things but it is primarily a discipline of holopoiesis, the creation of wholeness. Thus it focuses on both of the arms of the "L" and how they come together and interact. Incarnation is a process of creating this "L," this blending of spirit and earth within the person, turning a purely vertical or horizontal orientation into a partnership that embraces and acts within both in a holistic manner.

For this reason, while the specific practice and application of Incarnational Spirituality is shaped for each person by the unique nature of his or her individual life and circumstances, the overall practice is essentially the same for all of us. It is the practice of creating the "L," a practice of holopoiesis. It is a practice of creating the internal and external connections that allow the essential wholeness of creation and of the Sacred to emerge.

The Five Principles

Being aware of the five principles of incarnation—Identity, Boundary, Connection, Emergence, and Holopoiesis or the creation of wholeness—helps us see that incarnation is not an event but a process. It's an activity that we are engaged with every day as we live our lives and manifest our various projects. This awareness makes us more mindful that incarnation really is a practice, something we can develop and improve in ourselves and assist and empower in others.

For example, being aware of the principle of Identity encourages me to be more mindful of just who I am. What identity am I projecting into the world and why? What consequences unfold from such an identity? If I remember that my identity is a seed shape or core shape around which subtle energies form, much like flowing water taking on the shape of a boulder over and around which it flows, then I realize that in the application of this one principle lies an understanding of the art of manifestation. In fact, when I teach manifestation using the Manifestation Card Deck, one of the key steps is working out the clear identity of that which I'm trying to manifest.

Likewise with the principle of Boundary. What are my boundaries? How do I maintain and project them? Are they hard and fixed or are they fluid and permeable? What do I let into my life and what do I exclude, and why? Answering these kinds of questions can give me important insights into how I shape myself energetically and how I connect to my world. Similar self-reflective questions can be posed for all the principles as I seek to determine just how I engage with them and express them in my life.

The important part of these principles, particularly where the practice of Incarnational Spirituality is concerned, is that they are universal. We are all using them. They are like a common pool from which we all drink or a common bank of resources from which we all draw. Anything I do that blesses and improves that pool benefits all of us. If, for instance, I find ways of assisting and empowering your identity or I honor and respect your boundaries, or if I help you to be more connected or enable you to unfold and emerge out of your potentials—and especially if I can co-create wholeness with you—then I am not only helping you, I am also empowering the action of these principles within my own life. In simple terms, we are all co-incarnating together. If I help your incarnation, it cannot help but benefit my own. And this is true in a larger sense with all that I do to serve the incarnation of Gaia as reflected in the well-being of the world around me.

Two Applications

There are two particular applications of Incarnational Spirituality. One is a set of four practices that lie at the root of this approach, and the other is a set of four blessings that have emerged from it. These two applications, the Four Practices and the Four Blessings, truly sum up the essence of what Incarnational Spirituality is about and provide concrete activities that you can engage in to turn this from a set of ideas into a powerful daily practice.

The Four Practices and the Four Blessings are given in the Exercise section following this Chapter.

The Exercises

At the end of each of the previous chapters, I've suggested some exercises you can do. These exercises, or variants of them that you develop to fit the uniqueness of your own personal situation, can themselves become part of a practice of Incarnational Spirituality.

This is particularly true for the Presence Exercise which many of my students have made an element in their daily practice. Its purpose is to put us in touch with our own inner spirit of wholeness and the place where our own vertical and horizontal elements come together and blend. We could think of this place as the angle of the "L," formed by the meeting of its two arms. Our presence is the manifestation of the power of that meeting place and is a holopoietic force in its own right. We could call it our "Guardian Angle," pun intended!

The exercises can be divided into four broad categories. The first are broad, general exercises that establish the overall context for applying Incarnational Spirituality in your life. I include in this group the Four Practices and the Four Blessings given in the Exercise Section for this Chapter. Then there are the basic, core exercises such as Standing, Self-Light, and the Presence Exercise all of which work with establishing the felt sense of one's individual sovereignty and Self-Light. These form the foundation of Incarnational Spirituality. Then upon this foundation are built the exercises that work with subtle energies, the subtle environment, energy hygiene, and subtle activism. Finally, there are exercises of general attunement, particularly to Gaia. A list of exercises within each of these four categories is found in the Index of Exercises, as well as an alphabetized list of all the exercises in this book.

In crafting a personal spiritual practice using Incarnational

Spirituality, the place to start is with the foundational exercises, to which the others can be added as desired or needed. And once you have a sense of the overall objective of these exercises, you can use this to craft your own, for above all, Incarnational Spirituality honors uniqueness and freedom as you tailor a spiritual practice that honors your particular relationship to yourself, the world, and the Sacred.

A Unique Practice

Many spiritual traditions offer specific practices which a person can follow much like following a recipe. Incarnational Spirituality is different. It has its basic components as I have described, but its practice comes down to doing what you need to do to enable your life to be blessed and to be a blessing to the world. It's the practice of doing what enables you to be a source of empowerment and assistance to the incarnational process itself whether it's found in yourself, in a tree, in the company your work for, in the people around you, and in the world at large. It is a practice of mindfulness in being a partner with the world, a co-incarnate and a co-creator, an agent of wholeness.

What this means to you and how you manifest it in the particularity of your own life is a matter only you can determine. Ultimately, Incarnational Spirituality is a unique practice, one that you craft in freedom and awareness to be an expression of your innate sacredness giving itself to the world. It is an expression of your unique "Gaian Relationship." The two arms of the "L" of Incarnational Spirituality can be seen as "Individuality" and "Community," but how they meet and blend and manifest wholeness within your own personhood is something only you can shape and determine.

Learning Incarnational Spirituality is like discovering and learning the components of a toolbox and how to use them to good effect. But what you build with those tools is up to you. That is your personal gift to the world, something no one else can give. That is the essence of your unique practice.

In the end, the practice of Incarnational Spirituality is YOU.

EXERCISES FOR CHAPTER SIX

THE FOUR PRACTICES

All my life I have been aware of the subtle worlds and have had contact with various non-physical beings. As a child I took this awareness for granted and thought it perfectly normal. When I was twenty years old, I felt a calling to use this inner contact as the basis for researching the nature of the connections and interactions between the physical and subtle worlds—the place where the vertical and horizontal aspects of our lives merge to form the "L." At that time I was contacted by a specific subtle being whom I called "John" who said he would partner me in this endeavor; we entered into a collaboration that lasted for twenty-seven years during which John became a mentor and a colleague. I tell the story of my training and work with John in my book Apprenticed to Spirit.

At the beginning of our relationship when he was helping me to refine and further develop my connections with the subtle worlds, he gave me four practices to do on a daily basis. These were:

1. Attunement to Self
2. Attunement to Sacred
3. Attunement to the subtle worlds
4. Blessing the world around me

Each of these practices was composed of several elements. For instance, by "Attunement to Self," John meant self-reflection, self development, self-understanding, and anything else that would enable me to honor my sovereignty and uniqueness and be a more integrated and whole individual. In effect, this is my personal practice of Identity. "Attunement to the Sacred" meant any contemplative discipline that enabled me to attune to what was larger and vaster than my personal identity, such as my soul, the transpersonal, the Universal , Spirit, and Sacredness as the Ground of Being.

When John first gave me these practices, attunement to the subtle worlds specifically meant attuning to him twice a day every day as we worked over a matter of weeks to build up our unique relationship. Then it became expanded to mean a practice of attunement to the subtle half of the world, including the immediate subtle environment around all of us that is really an invisible part of the physical world and the subtle worlds that exist in dimensions beyond the physical. But this third practice could also be expanded further to mean simply a practice of sensitivity to the world, physical or non-physical, in which we live, that is to say, a mindful awareness of what is happening around us and those who inhabit the world with us.

Blessing meant any number of practices such as kindness or compassionate engagement that represented an effort to make the world a better place and to enhance the well-being of others.

These four practices became the foundation for insights that later evolved to become Incarnational Spirituality. They constituted a way of forming the "L," the integrated blending of the horizontal and vertical components of our lives. They remain a cornerstone for the overall application of Incarnational Spirituality in everyday life.

How you use these four practices is up to you. They are really categories more than specific practices in themselves. But they remind us of the different elements in our lives that contribute to our wholeness and of our connection to a larger world to which we bear responsibility.

THE FOUR BLESSINGS

The Four Blessings did not originate with John but come out of my later work with Incarnational Spirituality. However, they are ways of implementing the fourth practice, that of blessing the world around us as well as being a blessing for ourselves. These blessings are:

- Blessing the place you're in
- Blessing the people you're with
- Blessing yourself
- Blessing the work you're doing or the activity you're undertaking

121

Blessing can take different forms, but fundamentally I think of it as an act of holding. Thus to bless the place I'm in is a matter of holding my immediate environment in love, in honor, in appreciation, and mindfulness. The same for the people I'm with, for my work, and for myself.

In effect, part of blessing, at least, is holding the perception of the innate holopoietic impulse within all things—the desire of all beings for wholeness, which includes such qualities as safety, happiness, and fulfillment of their potentials—and being mindful of what I can do in the moment to advance the manifestation of that wholeness in the particular situation I find myself.

But blessing can take any form you care to give it or are able to give it. The real core of this practice is the awareness that blessing is possible, desirable, and that you are able to provide it. It is a way of seeing yourself as a force for good in your environment, thus fulfilling one of the intents of your soul in initiating your incarnation in the first place.

David Spangler lives in the Northwest, is married and has four children. Since 1965, he has worked clairvoyantly and intuitively with a group of non-physical beings from the inner worlds of spirit. They identified themselves as being part of an inner school whose purpose was to explore and develop a spiritual teaching around the process of incarnation. This teaching is intended to empower incarnate persons living in the physical world—individuals such as you and me—to lead lives of greater blessing and capacity and to be sources of blessing and service for the world as a whole. From 1970-1973, David was a co-director of the Findhorn Foundation Community in Northern Scotland. In 1974 he co-founded the Lorian Association, a non-profit spiritual educational organization, and continues to work with it today. David is also a Fellow of the Lindisfarne Association, a gathering of scientists, mathematicians, artists, spiritual and religious teachers, ecologists, and political scientists, all interested in promoting a new culture based on holistic and Gaian values. For further information on his work, writings and classes, please visit www.lorian.org.

NEXT STEPS

If the ideas and practice of Incarnational Spirituality interest you, here are some resources you can use to explore them more deeply. Most can be found in the Bookstore on the Lorian Website at www.Lorian.org.

Books

Apprenticed to Spirit: The Education of a Soul, by David Spangler; Riverhead Books (2011)

The Gathering Light, by Jeremy Berg; Lorian Press (2010)

Facing the Future, by David Spangler; Lorian Press (2010)

Subtle Worlds: An Explorer's Field Notes, by David Spangler; Lorian Press (2010)

[There will be additional books coming out that expand on the chapters in this Introduction. Check the Lorian Website for announcements when these books are available.]

Card Decks

The Soul's Oracle, by David Spangler and Jeremy Berg; Lorian Press (2011)

The Manifestation Deck, by David Spangler and Deva Berg; Lorian Press (2004)

Audio

Being Particular, by David Spangler; a lecture on CD available from the Lorian Bookstore

Publications   [Subscribe at www.lorian.org.]

David's Desk, a free monthly essay on spirituality and current events by David Spangler sent to all on the Lorian mailing list.

The View from the Borderlands, a quarterly journal by David Spangler and others on esoteric and spiritual topics, available by subscription only.

Self-Study Modules And Textbooks

The Lorian Association presents a number of self-study modules on various topics of Incarnational Spirituality plus textbooks that are published transcripts of classes by David Spangler; these are all available from the Lorian Website.

The Lorian Library

The Lorian Library is a source of further information. The Lorian Association has offered a Masters of Spiritual Direction degree and a Masters of Contemporary Spirituality. There are a number of theses written by graduate students for their degrees that can be found in the Library on the Lorian Website. The Library has other articles as well. These all throw light on Incarnational Spirituality and its applications as well in a variety of fields.

Classes

Lorian offers classes in Incarnational Spirituality and its applications. Please check the Lorian Website to see what is available.

Group Classes

If you would like to gather and sponsor a group to study some aspect of Incarnational Spirituality, please contact the Lorian office at info@Lorian.com to see what can be arranged.

Lorian Press
2204 E Grand Ave.
Everett, WA 98201

CPSIA information can be obtained at www.ICGtesting.com
Printed in the USA
BVOW010309280911

272301BV00001B/1/P